Building Connections Between **LITERACY** and **NUMERACY**

Building Connections Between **LITERACY** and **NUMERACY**

What If Your **ABC**s Were Your **123**s?

LESLIE MINTON

SAGE | AdvantEDGE Teacher Resources

Originally published in 2007 by

CORWIN
A SAGE Company

Corwin
A SAGE Company
2455 Teller Road
Thousand Oaks, CA 91320
www.corwin.com

This SAGE AdvantEdge edition published in 2014 by

SAGE | AdvantEDGE Teacher Resources

SAGE Publications India Pvt Ltd
B1/I-1 Mohan Cooperative Industrial Area
Mathura Road
New Delhi 110 044, India

Exclusively distributed in South Asia by

O·V·E·R·L·E·A·F

OVERLEAF
B 519 A Sushant Lok1
Gurgaon 122 002, India
email: overleaf@vsnl.net
www.overleaf.co.in

Second Printing 2015

Published by Vivek Mehra for SAGE Publications India Pvt Ltd and printed at Sai Print-o-Pack, New Delhi..

ISBN: 978-81-321-1618-9 (PB)

Contents

Contents

Preface

I am officially a lover of math! This is a very new stance for me, as I neither loved nor "got" math throughout my own school career. I remember doing well, in that my report card said I did, but I never felt comfortable with or sure of most of the procedures and tricks I supposedly learned. I don't think I am alone in my experiences.

During my formal training to become a teacher, I was required to take a single math methods course. With that and my prior experience, I felt confident that I could at the very least replicate my own level of understanding and teach math successfully to my future students. I have come to realize what a naive thought this was.

While my math studies were limited, my language arts studies were bountiful. My practicum and student teaching experiences focused on reading and writing; my cooperating teachers shared wonderful instructional strategies with great enthusiasm for the subject matter. Upon graduation, I felt well prepared to help students become readers and writers but not as prepared to help them become mathematicians. To be fair, I didn't know what I didn't know about math.

As a mathematics consultant providing professional development for elementary teachers, I learned that my teacher preparation was similar to what many of my colleagues experienced. Many elementary teachers confess a lack of confidence and competence in teaching mathematics as intentionally and as thoroughly as they teach reading. Even now, as I consult with K–8 teachers and administrators, I relate strongly to the teacher who is confident in her or his readiness to teach literacy but feels less prepared with strategies for math.

In 1983, the National Commission on Excellence in Education published the report *A Nation at Risk*, spurring conversations across the educational landscape. The questions were clear: "What should be done?" The answers were not as clear.

Researchers and educators began to focus on pedagogy and content in order to define effective practice. Much of this work was funded through the Elementary and Secondary Education Act (ESEA) enacted in 1965. The most significant sweeping education reform since then has been the No Child Left Behind Act of 2001 (NCLB), which is meant to increase accountability for student achievement results, expand flexibility and local control, and emphasize effective teaching methods in the areas of reading and math.

Since 1985, due to *A Nation at Risk*, educators, policy makers, the business community, and others have focused on developing a more comprehensive understanding of how reading is taught and learned. Researchers and organizations have worked to unpack what it means to be a good reader and articulated developmentally appropriate stages of reading to aid classroom teachers in creating materials and experiences that move readers to identified levels of proficiency. The outcome of this push has been that as a profession, we better understand the process and content of reading as well as the developmental learning path students take to become effective readers. Colleges and universities now provide prospective teachers with many opportunities to examine and practice effective teaching strategies and to broaden their understanding of the developmental aspects of reading.

So what about math? How can we begin to address this subject with the same rigor and commitment? If NCLB holds educators accountable for student achievement results in mathematics as well as reading, it makes sense that we consider what we've learned about reading.

I propose that we should build upon the years of work regarding literacy and make direct and purposeful connections to numeracy. This book is a beginning toward making those connections. By building on what we've learned about literacy development over the past 20 years and extending it to numeracy, we increase the likelihood that teachers and students will become lifetime lovers, "getters," and users of mathematics. The question remains: How can we discover what it is we don't know about numeracy so that we can create experiences for students that enable them to become numerate?

We need to begin to build in elementary schools the capacity to uncover the developmental path students take to build competence and confidence in themselves as mathematicians. I propose that by comparing literacy instruction with mathematics instruction, we can help teachers develop their own confidence and competence and increase their capacity to learn and teach mathematics. It is my intent in this book to begin that process and start the conversations.

Acknowledgments

Writing this book has been a collaborative effort; many people have contributed great wisdom and insight during the process, and bits and pieces of many people's experiences have been woven together to create the whole.

I do so appreciate the support and encouragement of my family and friends, who kept asking, "Are you done yet?"

Thank you, Samantha, Tucker, JanWillem, Judy, Tracy, Tori, Jeannie, Stephenie, Peter, Than, Mark, Ken, Alyssa, Kathryn, Stephen, Ryan, Tobias, Sophie, Elias, Amelia, Cynthia, and Andrea.

I also want to thank my colleague Mary Sanborn for her feedback and edits. I highly value your opinion.

Last, I want to acknowledge all of my former students and teaching colleagues, without whom I would have no experience to draw from.

The contributions of the following reviewers are gratefully acknowledged:

Deborah Gordon
Classroom Teacher
Phoenix, Arizona

Catherine Hernandez
National Board Certified Teacher
Detroit Public Schools
Detroit, Michigan

About the Author

Leslie Minton is a mathematics project director for the Maine Mathematics and Science Alliance in Augusta, Maine. She is also a codirector of the Teacher Student Learning Continuum, a project funded in part by an award from the Maine Department of Education, which provides financial and technical assistance to five Maine school districts. She is the project director for the Early Mathematical Thinking project (EMT), a collaboration among 25 Maine school sites engaging in a pilot of both a professional development course and program assessment materials centered on the mathematical development of K–4 students. She is a fellow of the second cohort group of Governor's Academy for Science and Mathematics Educators. She has taught regular and special education for Grades 4 through 12. Leslie received her BS in elementary and special education from the University of Maine at Farmington and her MEd in curriculum, instruction, and assessment from Walden University. She is coauthor of *Uncovering Student Thinking in Mathematics*.

I dedicate this book to the memory of my father, Stephen Sala, who believed in Attention Days, Great-to-Be-Alive Drives, and me.

I also dedicate this book to my mother, Judy Sala, who knows the Avis in me.

1 What If?

This book is a compilation of the lessons I've learned in my quest to become a better teacher and learner of mathematics. My purpose is to share my research, my experiences, and the experiences of my colleagues and peers to demonstrate how literacy and numeracy are similar, and thereby to influence classroom instruction for mathematics. One of my assumptions is that while a vast number of elementary teachers feel proficient and competent in teaching reading, not many of them have the same level of comfort or confidence in teaching mathematics. The reasons for this are varied, but the implications for teaching and learning are significant. How can we build on teachers' literacy strengths to help them teach and learn math? This book will take a look at current literacy instructional strategies and give examples of how they could be used in the teaching of mathematics.

Roland Barth (2003) defines the purpose of reflection as "nothing less than an internal dialogue with oneself. It is the process of bringing past experiences to a conscious level, analyzing them, and determining better ways to think and behave in the future" (p. xxi). It is in looking back while looking ahead that educators can continue to refine, revise, and in some cases overhaul their practices.

This book is meant to be a tool for reflection, helping you gain a new perspective based on the premise that mathematics and reading are more alike than different. I have paused in specific places to pose questions that encourage those reflective moments and give you an opportunity to relate to the text through your own experiences—to have your internal dialogue. Please use the spaces provided to document your thinking.

MAKING SENSE

Let's begin with the big picture to gain some perspective on our current reality. Does this scenario sound familiar?

You are at a dinner party, and during a conversation about the rising price of gasoline, someone asks how many miles per gallon people's vehicles get. As the comments move around the room, one person responds, "I have no idea about the miles per gallon my car gets and the current gas prices. I was never good at math!" Everyone smiles politely, some shake their heads in agreement, and others say aloud, "I was never good at math either."

Somehow there is consolation in acknowledging the lack of mathematical ability among adults. But imagine this scenario as the conversation continues:

As the conversation builds, someone refers to a recent article in Time *concerning alternative energies and their potential for lessening our dependence on foreign oil. As opinions are shared, one person responds, "I have no idea about the article or possible alternate sources of energy. I was never good at reading!"*

Suddenly the room becomes very quiet; there is no agreement.

Why is it that as a society we're willing to freely admit that we're not competent mathematicians but would disguise any struggle we had with being literate? What if we decided that numeracy and literacy are both languages we should be fluent in?

Can you think of how numeracy and literacy might be alike?

Marilyn Burns describes math as an American phobia "right up there with snakes, public speaking, and heights" (1998, p. ix). Commonly expressed sentiments about mathematics perpetuate the myth that real mathematical understanding is available to a limited number of people. Burns gives examples of these expressions:

> "Only some people are good in math."
>
> "You're only good in math if you have the math gene."
>
> "People who are good in math wear thick eyeglasses and plastic pocket protectors." (p. ix)

These negative beliefs and assumptions have permeated our culture and, in effect, have limited people in their daily lives and had long-term consequences on their livelihood. Because innumeracy in today's world deprives students of opportunity as well as competence in everyday tasks, it is vital that students understand the mathematics they're learning.

In the United States, there are currently 80 million workers whose everyday responsibilities require the use of basic Grade 6 arithmetic. Because many workers' computation skills are limited, some businesses have added pictures of meal orders to cash registers or provided registers that indicate correct change to cut down on calculation errors. By doing so, however, we deprive people of the necessity to actively think about the numbers involved in the transaction and thus further limit their real-world application of mathematics. Have you ever presented a clerk with money after he or she has entered an amount into the register and observed how stunned that person was by the need to personally calculate the change? To reverse this current direction, it is imperative that we begin to expect more from ourselves as educators and from our students as mathematicians.

Mathematical literacy involves more than proper execution of procedures; it requires a knowledge base and the competence and confidence to apply this knowledge in the practical world. A mathematically literate person can solve day-to-day problems, make estimations, interpret data, reason numerically, and communicate using mathematics. As our knowledge expands and the economy evolves, more people are working with technologies or in settings where mathematics is foundational. Processing of information, problem solving, and using numbers and symbols to communicate are becoming routine job requirements.

Conversations between the business community and educators reveal that expectations for student numeracy are similar to those shared for student literacy. Business leaders are looking for employees with pertinent mathematical skills:

- A strong number sense, including the ability to estimate and judge the reasonableness of an answer and to demonstrate fluency and flexibility when engaging in situations dependent on mathematical understanding
- Confidence in using different methods to measure time, money, length, etc.; experience using appropriate tools to do so; and a level of accuracy in the measurement and computation
- Familiarity with functions, change, variation; a strong spatial sense, including the ability to find routes on maps and to visualize problems
- Statistical and logical reasoning skills—the ability to support or justify arguments and the ability to explore and compare alternate strategies for solving problems

The workplace is one arena requiring mathematical understanding and proficiency, but the larger arena is outside the workplace. Mathematics is a part of everyday life, and therefore we all need to have a certain level of confidence and competence in our use of it to successfully navigate our world. Whether we're in the grocery store deciding which product is a better deal, at dinner adding up our portion of the tab or figuring the tip, in the convenience store trying to determine whether the clerk gave us the correct change, or contemplating which apartment we can afford if we make $100 per week, we all rely on everyday mathematics when we make daily decisions. Mathematical literacy is one of the keys to coping with a changing society, and we as educators need to consider how we're preparing students for the real world.

In its report *Helping Children Learn Mathematics* (2002), the National Research Council (NRC) shares its findings on the teaching and learning of elementary school mathematics. The report argues for an instructional goal of "mathematical proficiency," a broader outcome than that of mere procedural knowledge. The report further suggests that a balance of five intertwined strands comprising the idea of mathematical proficiency should guide the teaching of mathematics. Emphasizing one strand and expecting that the others will develop as a result of this singular focus has been ineffective in supporting mathematical proficiency. Weaving the strands together by connecting ideas and developing overall understanding forms a solid structure from which to build more sophisticated ideas and increase mathematical proficiency.

The NRC defines these five strands as follows:

1. Conceptual understanding—comprehension of mathematical concepts, operations, and relationships
2. Procedural fluency—skill in carrying out procedures flexibly, accurately, efficiently, and consistently
3. Strategic competence—ability to formulate, represent, and solve mathematical problems in a variety of contexts

4. Adaptive reasoning—capacity for logical thought, reflection, and explanation and justification of one's thinking

5. Productive engagement—ability and inclination to see mathematics as sensible, doable, and worthwhile

In considering these five strands as necessary to the building of an effective mathematics experience for students, we must begin to look more closely at teacher instruction. "Despite the common myth that teaching is little more than common sense or that some people are just born teachers, effective teaching practice can be learned" (NRC, 2001, p. 369).

What are some ways that you use mathematics in your everyday life? How do they relate to the content you teach?

A CHANGING LANDSCAPE

Society has always valued literacy. If we are to navigate the endless maze of communication that faces us daily, it is imperative that we understand written and spoken words. Literacy is an important factor in determining student success, and we have spent much time and money at the local and federal levels in an effort to raise a nation of literate citizens. Isn't it enough, then, if students can read? Do they really need to be numerate?

Have you had access to quality professional development in mathematics during the past 5 years?

According to Robert Ashlock, we are a society "drenched with data" (2002, p. 3). Technology is changing our world, and quantitative literacy, or numeracy, is now essential for making sense of the landscape. Students' experiences and instruction need to reflect these changes. Our instruction must enable students to become mathematically proficient so that they are prepared for the real world.

In 1989, the National Council of Teachers of Mathematics (NCTM) stated, "Today's society expects schools to insure that all students have an opportunity to become mathematically literate, are capable of extending their learning, have an equal opportunity to learn, and become informed citizens capable of understanding issues in a technological society" (p. 3).

> In this changing world, those who understand and can do mathematics will have significantly enhanced opportunities and options for shaping their futures. Mathematical competence opens doors to productive futures. A lack of mathematical competence keeps those doors closed.
>
> —NCTM, *Principles and Standards for School Mathematics*, p. 5

Educators and researchers recognize that while articulating what should be learned is essential, so is articulating how it should be taught, and the NCTM continued its work in an effort to better articulate goals for both the teaching and the learning of mathematics. The *Principles and Standards for School Mathematics* (NCTM, 2000) and the *Research Companion* (NCTM, 2003) further elucidated the important concepts and processes all mathematically proficient students need to acquire by Grade 12.

We need to develop experiences for students that will enable them to value mathematics and feel confident and competent in their abilities to reason, solve problems, and communicate their thinking. These aspirations for students are certainly parallel to what we want them to learn from their reading experiences.

In the past two decades, a number of systems, programs, tools, and mandates have been implemented to encourage our students to become confident and capable readers—to value reading, to solve problems by using strategies to understand text, and to communicate by understanding, inferring from, and reflecting on the written word. We now need to begin developing systems, programs, tools, and resources at local, state, and federal levels to support numeracy with the same vigor. I suggest that if we can recognize the similarities in the disciplines, we are closer to creating a nation of mathematically literate citizens. If we build on what we as elementary teachers know to be sound instructional practices for literacy, we can become more effective in providing sound instructional practices for numeracy.

The remainder of this book will explore the connections between the disciplines to help further uncover the developmental growth involved in becoming numerate and the instructional implications of this. Chapter 2 will focus on how students become proficient in literacy and numeracy by giving an analysis of the processes and structures of both content areas. Chapter 3 moves into the realm of understanding and comprehension, and Chapter 4 looks specifically at developmental stages of mathematical understanding and procedural and conceptual knowledge. Finally, Chapter 5 provides examples of how teachers are making use of these connections in their classrooms and gives you some ideas to try in your own classroom.

2

What Do Good Readers and Mathematicians Look Like?

To develop an informed citizenry and to support a democratic government, schools must graduate students who are numerate as well as literate.

—U.S. Department of Education, www.ed.gov

Before we begin discussing the similarities between literacy and numeracy, we must uncover what good mathematicians and readers look like so we can find a core of beliefs that pertain to both disciplines.

When students are asked in the classroom to describe "good mathematicians," they often describe them the same way they describe good readers, giving responses far more pertinent to literacy than to numeracy. The following picture demonstrates how students who haven't had opportunities to think and talk about what they're doing in mathematics will generalize rules from literacy that are not as important in mathematics.

Figure 2.1 Student Responses to the Question, What Do Good Mathematicians Do?

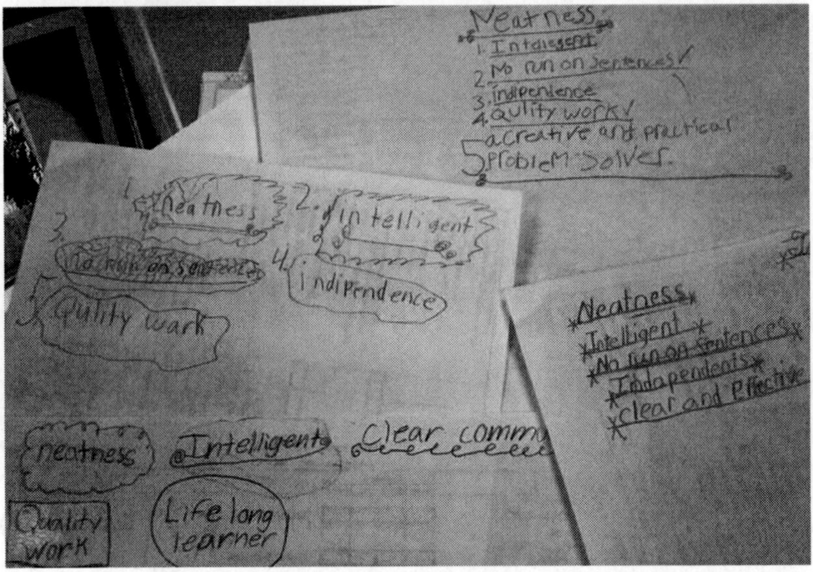

Figure 2.2 One Student's Response to the Question, What Do Good Mathematicians Do? Following More Specific Focus on Mathematics

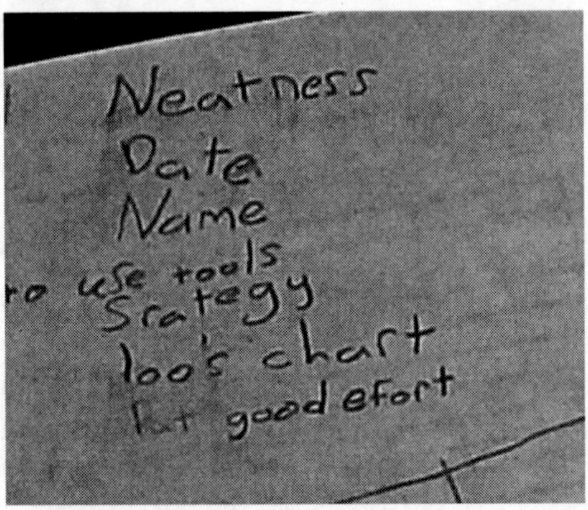

In this particular third-grade classroom, the teacher encouraged his students to think about what they were doing when they engaged in mathematical activities. He had them work on some investigations, record their findings, and share ideas, and then brought them back together to have another conversation. This time, some students were able to relate a little more to what they were doing in math class.

Over the next week the teacher continued to provide opportunities for reflection and discussion of the question, What do good mathematicians do? By continuing to have his students articulate their own thinking, he set the stage so that they would be able to monitor their own behaviors and grow as mathematicians.

It's important to revisit these ideas with your students throughout the year so that they can reflect on new understandings and

Figure 2.3 A Third-Grade Reflection of Current Understanding

refine their knowledge. The more students can articulate what good mathematicians do, the more they'll be able to practice these behaviors and internalize them for their own use.

As students practice identifying attributes and characteristics of good mathematicians, they become more aware of themselves as learners. They begin to recognize and describe behaviors associated with good habits, and they become more able to think of themselves as succeeders who can meet identified standards.

The following table gives examples of behaviors students list when they describe what good mathematicians do and compares them to those Irene Fountas and Gay Su Pinnell (2000) found students commonly identify as behaviors of good readers. (Please note that these lists are placed side by side so that they may be compared, but this is not meant to imply that items adjacent to each other are necessarily parallel.)

Table 2.1 Student-Identified Characteristics of Good Mathematicians and Readers

Good Mathematicians	*Good Readers*
Use pictures, words, and numbers to explain their thinking (*represent/model their thinking*)	Choose "just right" books (*practice at an appropriate level*)
Know facts (*have automatic or systematic fact knowledge*)	Sound out letters and words (*break apart the whole into parts/strategies*)
Think hard about problems (*engage with the mathematics*)	Show thinking while reading (*engage with the text*)
Know there is more than one way to solve a problem (*are flexible and efficient; use multiple strategies*)	Use schema to understand and interpret text (*are flexible and efficient; use prior knowledge*)

Of course, these lists are student generated and are not intended to be complete or "the list." Students in different age groups will be influenced differently, depending on what their prior experiences in math have been. For example, students who have been repeatedly given timed fact tests will equate math with knowing facts, while those who have grappled with robust problems in relevant contexts may relate to "Think hard about problems." Students can't articulate what they haven't seen, heard, or done. Teachers can help students by providing them with a variety of math activities and opportunities to discuss mathematical processes as well as the answers, letting them see value in both and therefore sharpening their understanding of what it means to be a good mathematician.

WORDS INTO ACTIONS

The idea that it's important for students to identify behaviors before they progress to making sense of the content is based on beliefs about the development of mathematical knowledge.

Educational research offers compelling evidence that students learn math well only when they construct their own understanding by engaging with the mathematics (Ginsberg, 1989; Kamii, 1989; Yackel, Cobb, Wood, Wheatley, & Merkel, 1990).

Constructivism is not a new term or idea, but its use as a pedagogical approach is increasing as educators and researchers find that students have an innate developmental logic to their thinking, which, when engaged, allows for the expression of mathematical understanding. When children are encouraged to develop their own ideas based on their experiences and knowledge, they are able to "construct" meaning better than they are if they don't interact with the ideas in a meaningful way. Readers take their existing knowledge (schema) and put it together with new information they encounter in text to construct meaning as they read. Similarly, mathematicians construct meaning by using mathematical reasoning to develop their own strategies and approaches. Instruction based on the idea of constructing knowledge provides opportunity and gives purpose to students' work.

How do you support your students in constructing their own meaning in literacy? In mathematics? Are there any similarities?

Reading is a complex, multifaceted process that begins and ends with making meaning of text. Readers rely on strategies derived from conventional rules of print and use their schema to enhance their understanding. Young readers develop greater confidence in constructing their understanding by working with stories that become increasingly more difficult to read as they go along. Students are presented with text of varied structure, organization, and subject matter.

Similarly, mathematics is a process that begins and ends with making meaning of numbers. Mathematicians rely on efficient and accurate strategies to lead them to successful solution of problems, and these strategies become more sophisticated the more they have access to challenging problems. The variations and complexities they encounter require them to choose appropriate strategies and find different ways of thinking about problems.

> Being numerate involves having those concepts and skills of mathematics that are required to meet the demands of everyday life. It includes having the capacity to select and use them appropriately

> in real settings. Being truly numerate requires the knowledge and disposition to think and act mathematically and the confidence and intuition to apply particular mathematical principles to everyday problems. (*Essential Learnings Framework 1*, 2003, p. 21)

Let's look at how the structures of reading and mathematics can be aligned. The concepts competent readers and competent mathematicians understand and the skills they possess are put together in Table 2.2 so that you can begin thinking about how these disciplines are related through similar structures. The surface structures refer to skills and skill sets necessary for successful application of the deep structures, which are the concepts and processes students must grasp in order to succeed.

Using language often used to describe cognition involved in literacy development, this table illustrates connections between reading and math. By examining these structures, teachers will be more able to recognize instructional strategies that can be used interchangeably.

As we begin a closer comparison of literacy and numeracy, it is important to realize that both involve developmental acquisition of skills and concepts. In the remainder of this chapter, we will look at the similarities through that developmental lens and consider instructional strategies that work well for both content areas. I should mention that while my focus is on the similarities for the purpose of building connections, recognition of instructional and structural differences between the content areas will improve our understanding of how to teach mathematics.

LITERACY

How do students become good readers? We have certainly done a great deal over the past 20 years to define what good readers look like and have thereby produced instruction that more effectively supports students' learning. Educators have delineated stages of development that students move through as a result of their experiences and understanding in order to make sense of text and read.

Table 2.2 Structure Systems of Reading and Mathematics

Surface Structure Systems		*Deep Structure Systems*	
Reading	*Mathematics*	*Reading*	*Mathematics*
Letter/Sound Awareness (Graphophonic) (phonemic awareness—e.g., *A* says "a" as in *apple*)	**Digit/Value/Name Awareness** (digit awareness—e.g., *1* says "one"; it is the numeral 1 and represents one object)	**Semantic** (understanding the meanings of words and how words differ from symbols)	**Semantic** (understanding the meanings of numbers and how numbers differ from symbols)
Decoding (Graphophonic) (isolating letter sounds, maintaining them, and putting them together to form a word—e.g., "k" + "a" + "t" = "cat")	**Taking Numbers Apart by Digits** (combining digits for total value/ recognizing place value—e.g., 12 = 3 + 3 + 3 + 3 or 6 + 6; 5 = 3 + 2)	**Schematic** (constructing meaning at the whole text level; using prior knowledge to enhance understanding)	**Schematic** (constructing meaning at the whole number/ contextual level; using prior knowledge to enhance understanding)
Visual Word Recognition (Lexical) (creating an automatic response to seeing words)	**Visual Number Fact Recognition** (creating an automatic response to seeing simple problems)	**Pragmatic** (reading for specific purposes and audiences)	**Pragmatic** (using mathematics for specific purposes, especially practical ones—e.g., determining whether a problem requires an estimate or an exact answer)
Syntactic (recognizing and using the rules and patterns of syntax—i.e., language structure at the word, sentence, and text levels)	**Syntactic** (recognizing and using the rules and patterns of our base 10 number system and basic math operations)		

Since the No Child Left Behind Act (NCLB) was passed in 2001, however, legislation has focused our nation's attention and resources on creating an assessment-driven system that all too often produces high-stakes tests rather than seeks to improve content and pedagogy. According to the U.S. Department of Education (2004), we now spend $501.3 billion annually on elementary and secondary education. American taxpayers invest more in education than they do in the Department of Defense, and the U.S. spends more per pupil than almost any other nation in the world. Unfortunately, as noted by Barry McGaw, education director of the Organization for Economic Development, "The U.S. doesn't get the bang for its buck" (¶ 2).

If we build on the research base constructed over the last 20 years to define reading in developmental stages, we'll be better able to identify students' current levels of performance and therefore better able to design instruction to help them meet developmental milestones and become proficient readers.

What does being literate mean to you? How do your students demonstrate that they are literate?

Simply put, reading is thinking about text—but the task of reading is anything but simple. Reading requires the mind to process information from many different sources simultaneously and to make meaning of those words. The moment our eyes fall on a word, a complex set of processes is set in motion. Nerve impulses from the eyes stimulate an area near the back of the brain that allows us to see the light and dark areas on a page that define each letter. This is also how we recognize numerals. A region of the brain farther forward allows us to convert the letters we see into sounds and those sounds into language. The same region allows us to convert the numerals we see into their language sounds—that is, the names of numbers. Finally, another part of the brain converts the jumble of words in any given sentence into something meaningful. Likewise, this part of the brain allows us to identify numerals, determine their place in sequence, and interpret what quantity or value they represent.

Understanding explicit material on the page—letters, numbers, words, spaces, symbols, and pictures—and understanding what's implied (that is, the author's purpose) are challenging skills on their own. However, it is the merging of the explicit and the implied that ultimately allows a reader to make sense of text. To bring the page to life, students need purposeful instruction on the way sounds and letters create words and ideas and meaningful, enriching practice with text. Readers at all stages need immersion in high-quality reading material in a variety of genres.

Learning to read is a sequential process; each new skill builds on the mastery of those previously learned. Each step relates to one of the three main components of reading: decoding, comprehension, and retention. Students work first with letters and sounds, then words, then sentences and paragraphs. By further breaking down these processes, we can look at the structures underlying the assimilation of language and see how these structures support students as they learn to read.

What are some strategies you use to help your students with the process of reading at their grade level?

Structures of Reading

Let's look more closely at the structure of reading. Reading is experienced through a sort of signal system in the brain. Theorists believe there are six channels, or cuing systems, that operate simultaneously to deliver a great deal of information from surface and deep structure systems. All six of these structure systems are required to help readers make sense of what they read. Surface structures enable readers to quickly and accurately identify and pronounce words as well as to recognize when words and sentences makes sense. Deep structure systems enable us to understand and remember what we've read and to interpret and analyze the material at both the literal and inferential levels. Readers learn to rely on different sources of information at different times, depending on the purpose and context of the reading. These structure systems are required for math as well as for reading, as they support the developmental path learners must take and provide a foundation for moving to more sophisticated content.

Surface structure systems present readers with visible and audible information about letters, sounds, words, and grammar. These systems are:

1. The graphophonic system, which provides information about letters, combinations of letters, and the sounds associated with the letters
2. The lexical system, which provides information about words, including sight words, but not necessarily the meanings of words
3. The syntactic system, which provides information about the form and structure of language, giving awareness of the structures of words, sentences, and whole texts and allowing readers to decide whether they "sound right"

Successful readers use these surface structure systems to develop certain skills:

1. Phonemic awareness—awareness of the sounds that form spoken words
2. Alphabetic knowledge—knowing how the sounds of our language relate to the letters of the alphabet
3. Word context awareness—knowing how each word fits into the sentence or surrounding text
4. Word recognition—developing a bank of words recognized automatically (sight vocabulary)
5. Word analysis—identifying parts of words (roots, prefixes, suffixes)
6. Rereading and reading ahead—noticing the flow of language and understanding the ideas of the text
7. Sentence and text structure awareness—understanding the way words are put together

Decoding

Phonemic awareness and alphabetic knowledge are the skills involved in decoding, the first component of reading. Children begin decoding when they become aware that letters represent the sounds of spoken words. As they move through the alphabet, recognizing each letter, they associate the sounds represented with the letters they are seeing. By breaking up words into their component sounds, or phonemes, they learn to sound out words. For instance, the three phonemes of *dog* are "d," "aw," and "g." Children learning to decode hear three sounds, not because the ear hears them that way (the ear hears one pulse of sound), but because the brain automatically separates them. As children practice reading, they begin to decode more automatically. They begin to see words and read them without struggling, even if they don't know the meaning of every word. Decoding is a foundation children need in order to read fluently.

> Students do not first learn to decode and then become readers; they must be engaged in reading, thinking about, and discussing interesting texts from the beginning.
>
> —Patricia Scharer et al., *Becoming an Engaged Reader,* p. 25

What instruction do you give your students to help them learn to decode? What makes a "good" decoder?

Comprehension

Decoding skills move children to the next component of the process: comprehension. Initially, students use the skills of word recognition to develop a sight vocabulary, or word bank, which is important in paving the way for the next step of comprehension. When word recognition becomes automatic, students are better able to concentrate on the meaning of whole sentences and paragraphs while they read. Students also develop the ability to simultaneously connect information within the text and to make connections to what they already know—their schema. A student's schema allows him or her to interact with the text on a personal level, thereby enhancing retention of information.

> **What instruction do you give your students to support comprehension?**

Retention

Retention—moving information into long-term memory so that it can be recalled later—is the final component of the reading process. To retain what they read, students must be able to organize and summarize the content and readily connect it to what they already know. We should encourage our students to use their schema to make text-to-text, text-to-self, and text-to-world connections. Activation of prior knowledge is crucial to effective reading comprehension and retention.

How do you use the idea of schema in your current instruction to support retention of ideas?

Now that we've taken a look at how children learn to read and become literate, let's move on to how children become numerate.

NUMERACY

How do students become numerate? Until NCLB, how to address the state of mathematics education in the United States received little interest, with perhaps the exception of the TIMSS project carried out by the International Association for the Evaluation of Educational Achievement (IEA). The TIMSS (Trends in International Mathematics and Science Study) has conducted international comparisons in education for the past decade. The most recent study evaluated fourth- and eighth-graders in some 46 countries on their achievement in math and science in order to uncover similarities and differences in instruction

> The Challenge: America's schools are not producing the math excellence required for global economic leadership and homeland security in the 21st century.
>
> —U.S. Department of Education, www.ed.gov

and identify effective teaching practices. The information gained from this work has been instrumental in focusing attention on the need for reform in mathematics instruction across the United States. While the results of the TIMSS studies highlight effective practices for teaching math, national and local funding have not been as forthcoming as they have been for literacy instruction and the impact of what was learned has been largely unrealized. That is, until now.

According to U.S. Secretary of Education Margaret Spellings, "To compete in the global economy, you must know math. Therefore it is more important than ever that our students receive solid math instruction in the early grades to prepare them to take and pass Algebra and other challenging courses in middle school and high school" (United States Department of Education, 2006).

Outlined in the Math Now initiative and captured in Table 2.3 are some findings that demonstrate our need to look more thoroughly at mathematics education globally in order to support our students locally. Global competition is compelling us to ensure that U.S. students have the benefit of a solid mathematics foundation.

Part of the $260 million dollars allocated for the Math Now initiative has gone to the creation of a National Mathematics Panel modeled after the National Reading Panel, which was very influential in determining effective instruction for literacy and creating research-based practices that have become the foundation of current reading curricula. Likewise, the National Mathematics Panel aims to look at current teaching practices to determine what effective mathematics instruction looks like and to create a research base that will help teachers improve their instruction.

> Over the last decade, researchers have scientifically proven the best ways to teach reading. We must do the same in math. That means using only research-based teaching methods and rejecting unproven fads.
>
> —U.S. Department of Education, www.ed.gov

Given this renewed focus, the time has come to build in our

Table 2.3 Findings Pertaining to Mathematics Education in the United States

To compete in the global economy of the 21st century, knowledge of math is critical. Today's high school graduates need to have solid math skills—whether they are proceeding directly to college, or going straight into the workforce. In today's changing world, employers seek critical thinkers and practical problem-solvers fluent in today's technology.
U.S. students are currently performing below their international peers on math and science assessments: • Only 7% of 4th and 8th graders achieved an advanced level on the 2003 Trends in International Math and Science Study (TIMSS) test, compared to 38% of Singaporean 4th graders and 44% of Singaporean 8th graders. • On the most recent Program for International Student Assessment (PISA), American 15-year-olds performed below the international average in mathematics literacy and problem solving.
Today, only 22 states and the District of Columbia require high school students to complete at least three years of math and three years of science, the minimum *A Nation at Risk* recommended more than 20 years ago.
An applicant for a production associate's job at a modern automobile plant has to have the math skills equivalent to the most basic achievement level on the National Assessment of Educational Progress (NAEP) math test to meet company proficiency requirements, a threshold that almost half of 17-year-olds do not meet.
As part of his American Competitiveness Initiative, President Bush is proposing $260 million for math programs that will focus on strengthening math education in the early grades and middle school so that students enter high school ready to take challenging coursework.

SOURCE: United States Department of Education, 2006.

schools professional development opportunities for teachers that will enable them to increase their knowledge of the developmental process of learning mathematics and understand how to teach it.

Remember that the positive results in literacy are a direct result of dedicating resources (that is, time and money) to discovering how children learn to read and providing teachers with frameworks and materials that support teaching and learning. Clearly, achieving similar results in mathematics will take time, but if we are able to draw from our understanding of literacy, we may sooner be able to positively impact mathematics education and become a nation of numerate people.

What does being numerate mean to you? What are some ways your students demonstrate that they are numerate?

The Process

Recently, researchers have examined aspects of the brain that are involved when children think with numbers. Most researchers agree that memory, language, attention, temporal-sequential ordering, higher-order cognition, and spatial ordering are among the neurodevelopmental functions that play a role when children think with numbers. These components become part of an ongoing process in which students constantly integrate new concepts and procedural skills as they solve more and more advanced math problems.

For students to succeed in mathematics, a number of brain functions need to work together. Students must be able to use memory to recall rules and formulas and recognize patterns; use language to understand vocabulary and instructions and explain their thinking; and use sequential ordering to solve multistep problems and follow procedures. In addition, they must use spatial ordering to recognize symbols and work with geometric forms. Higher-order cognition helps them review alternative strategies while solving problems, monitor their thinking, assess the reasonableness of their answers, and transfer and apply learned skills to new problems. Often, several of these brain functions need to operate simultaneously.

Like learning to read text, learning to read numbers requires the use of surface structures and the development of skill sets. Visual, physical, and audible information provide students with strategies to build an understanding of more sophisticated mathematical ideas.

The following skills are necessary for success in thinking mathematically:

1. Numeric awareness—awareness of the digits and their spoken names
2. Numeric knowledge—understanding what numerals are and the quantities they represent; knowing the value of each digit based on its position in relation to the rest of the number
3. Number context awareness—understanding how numbers, words, and operational signs are arranged in a problem
4. Number recognition—developing a bank of number facts recognized automatically or retrieved systematically
5. Number analysis—using knowledge of numbers to find solutions to problems instead of being directed by operational signs
6. Rereading and reading ahead—using the context to decide on strategies for solving word problems
7. Operational awareness—understanding relationships between numbers in a problem and how equations are put together

Table 2.4 puts the skills and strategies of literacy and numeracy side by side to illuminate the similarities.

Table 2.4 Student-Identified Characteristics of Good Mathematicians and Readers

Type of Skill	*Readers*	*Mathematicians*
Decoding	*Phonemic Awareness* – awareness of the sounds that form spoken words	*Numeric Awareness* – awareness of the digits and their spoken names
	Alphabetic Knowledge – knowing how the sounds of our language relate to the letters of the alphabet	*Numeric Knowledge* – understanding what numerals are and the quantities they represent; knowing the value of each digit based on its position in relation to the rest of the number
Comprehension	*Word Context Awareness* – knowing how each word fits into the sentence or surrounding text	*Number Context Awareness* – understanding how numbers and operational signs are arranged in a problem
	Word Recognition – developing a bank of words recognized automatically (sight vocabulary)	*Number Recognition* – developing a bank of number facts recognized automatically or retrieved systematically
Retention	*Word Analysis* – identifying parts of words (roots, prefixes, suffixes)	*Number Analysis* – using knowledge of numbers to find solutions to problems instead of being directed by operational signs
	Rereading and Reading Ahead – noticing the flow of language and understanding the ideas of the text	*Rereading and Reading Ahead* – using key words and context to decide on strategies for solving word problems
	Sentence and Text Structure Awareness – understanding the way words are put together	*Operational Awareness* – understanding relationships between numbers in a problem and how equations are put together

Do the skills and strategies outlined in Table 2.4 make sense to you? Does this help when you think about curriculum, instruction, and assessment decisions?

Learning to be numerate, like learning to be literate, is a sequential process; each new skill builds on an understanding and mastery of previously learned skills. To compare literacy with fluency in math, I will apply the three components of reading to numeracy.

nu*mer*a*cy (n)—competence in the mathematical skills needed to cope with everyday life and the understanding of information presented in mathematical terms like graphs, tables, or charts

—*Oxford American Dictionary*

Decoding

The skills involved in decoding—when we're talking about numeracy—are numeric awareness and numeric knowledge. Children begin to decode numbers when they learn to recite them in order. They can usually be taught to start at 1 and continue to 10 with some degree of success, but at this time they don't associate a quantity—unless, perhaps, it's one or two—with the symbol or the spoken name. Children learn to recite numbers in the same manner they learn to recite the alphabet; their knowledge of the correct order is dependent on rote memorization. We all know that LMNOP is not one letter, but for a while many children lop it together as one because they're simply reciting what they've heard others say and don't yet understand the significance of each letter. In the same way, children learning to say their numbers may not understand the significance of each digit.

Children move from this early numeric awareness to numeric knowledge by associating the quantity represented to the number they are hearing or seeing. They begin to make connections between the names of numbers by discovering the pattern of our base 10 number system. They also begin to recognize the parts of multidigit numbers by breaking them up into their individual digits. As children practice, they begin to decode more automatically. They begin to see numbers and say them without struggling, even if they don't know the value of every number they say. Decoding numbers is part of the foundation children need in order to become numerate.

What connections can you make between decoding in literacy and decoding in numeracy? Can you see instructional similarities as well?

Comprehension

Decoding skills move children to the next component of numeracy: comprehension. Students need to learn to understand written numbers and their relationships to each other, and they begin by using the skills of numeric recognition to develop a bank of number facts (for example, simple addition or subtraction facts). When number recognition becomes automatic, students are better able to concentrate on the meanings and relationships of numbers within problems by making connections to what they already know about numbers (their schema). They are thus able to contextualize numbers to the world around them.

Think about what comprehension means. How can you support your students' comprehension of our number system?

Retention

Retention—remembering what has been learned—is the last component of numeracy. A cycle of learning and retention begins when students start to analyze numbers and their representations.

As they develop fluency with facts and an understanding of our base 10 number system, they become able to generalize ideas and apply them in more sophisticated ways (using integers, fractions, decimals, percents, etc.) to solve problems. When students organize and summarize their thinking and connect it to what they already know and understand, they are moving information into their long-term memory in such a way that it can be recalled later. They then have the opportunity to activate prior knowledge and make number-to-number, number-to-self, and number-to-world connections, which support retention.

What are some instructional strategies you use to help your students retain mathematical information?

By comparing learning to read with learning to be numerate, we see that there are inherent likenesses that lend themselves to similar instructional strategies.

Let's move on to Chapter 3 and focus on the concept of understanding.

3 What Is Understanding?

As teachers, all of us want to make sure our students understand what they're learning. But before we can recognize how students demonstrate their understanding of mathematics, we need to have a clear idea of what understanding is.

How do you define understanding?

If you look up *understanding* in the dictionary, you will find that it is a synonym for *comprehension*. Because we're familiar with the term comprehension as it pertains to literacy, it makes sense to draw from our knowledge of reading comprehension in our efforts to develop a clearer concept of mathematical understanding.

Do you believe that mathematical comprehension involves the same depth of understanding as reading comprehension?

Reading comprehension refers to a student's mental grasp of written material. Teachers often have students demonstrate their comprehension of what they've read by asking them questions. The quality of the question drives the quality of the reader's response. For instance, a student may be able to recall isolated facts—such as the color of the main character's car—but this doesn't reveal the student's understanding of the meaning of the text. A reader makes meaning from both visual information—the print and illustrations—and nonvisual information—the background knowledge and experience he or she brings to the text. Therefore, careful consideration of schema and how it influences understanding is essential in helping readers make sense of text.

Table 3.1 presents strategies students can use to enhance their reading comprehension and compares them to strategies students can use to enhance their mathematical comprehension. Instruction that explicitly incorporates these strategies in either context prompts students to think about what they're doing and therefore enables them to be more self-directed and to monitor their own learning.

Table 3.1 Strategies to Enhance Comprehension

Literacy Strategies	*Numeracy Strategies*
Making Text-to-Self, Text-to-Text, and Text-to-World Connections—bringing personal knowledge and life experiences to text	**Making Number-to-Self, Number-to-Number, and Number-to-World Connections**—bringing personal knowledge and life experiences to numbers
Creating Mental Images—visually assimilating text through the mind's eye	**Creating Mental Images**—visually assimilating problems through the mind's eye
Expanding Vocabulary—understanding (receptive) and using (expressive) new words	**Expanding Vocabulary**—understanding (receptive) and using (expressive) mathematical terms
Asking Questions—actively thinking about what is read by asking questions and seeking answers in the text (metacognition)	**Asking Questions**—making sense of what one is doing by asking questions and seeking answers, and using this thinking to make decisions and solve problems (metacognition)
Determining Importance—giving conscious attention to deciding what is important in the text	**Determining Importance**—giving conscious attention to deciding what is important in a problem
Inferring—creating new meaning on the basis of life experiences and clues from the text	**Inferring**—creating new meaning on the basis of life experiences and clues from the context of problems
Synthesizing—delving deeper into the message of the text by considering how each part contributes to the whole	**Synthesizing**—combining ideas or models or strategies in a new way

As you look at Table 3.1, what is your first reaction? Have you thought of comprehension strategies for mathematics before? How can these strategies affect your instruction?

Mathematics is often referred to as a subject that students either understand or do not understand. In reality, mathematics is composed of a wide variety of skills and concepts that are connected by an understanding of number. Number knowledge is the foundation for all mathematics as letter knowledge is the foundation for all reading.

> The meaning does not reside in the numbers; the numbers reside in understanding the meaning.

While mathematics is sequential in its overall structure, students are apt to learn skills and concepts in a nonlinear fashion. This has great impact on teaching and learning in mathematics classrooms, as simply moving through chapters in the textbook often replicates the sequence without revealing much connection between concepts and skills. For instance, students who are visual-spatial learners and struggle with numbers may shine when the unit on geometry comes along because they can see the mathematics in the shapes, just as some readers rely solely on pictures and their memories to compensate for their weaker decoding skills.

Learning mathematics, like learning to read, is a developmental process. Students' understanding of numbers is not determined by, for

Figure 3.1 Counting Is More Than Reciting the Number Names in Order

example, their ability to recite numbers in order from 1 to 100, just as their understanding of the written word is not determined by their ability to recite the alphabet.

What are some ways that learning the alphabet and learning to count are similar? How do you decide whether your students have an understanding of either?

As we move into a deeper analysis of the comprehension strategies, it is important to note that these strategies are significant for learners in any context; true understanding is at the core of all teaching and learning. For the purposes of this book, however, I will talk about these strategies as they relate specifically to mathematics, making comparisons to literacy as appropriate.

The first strategy is *making connections*—helping students make direct and specific connections between themselves and mathematics. Number-to-self, number-to-number, and number-to-world connections provide evidence of the importance of numbers in our everyday lives. For instance, we might ask very young students to think about what the number five means to them. They may say things like: "I have five fingers on this hand" or "I have five brothers and sisters" or "I am five years old." All of these responses demonstrate a personal relationship to the number five and tell us that our students are connecting the word number with a specific quantity.

When we encourage our students to make connections, we need to consider their schema. Schema includes prior knowledge, patterns of discourse, and experiences in the world. Our awareness of the

Figure 3.2 Counting Is the Foundation

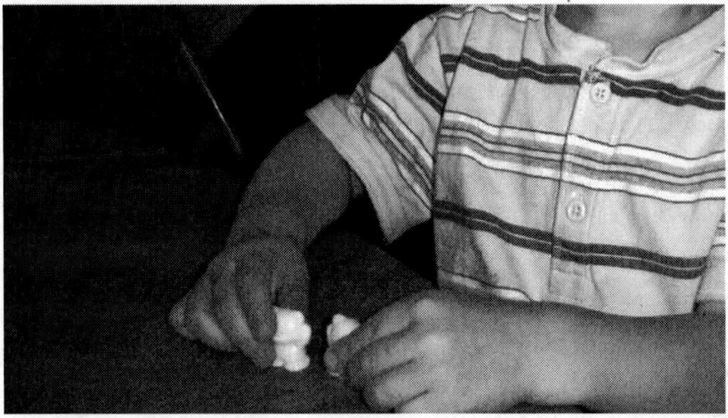

knowledge and understanding students bring with them to school is helpful in informing our instruction. Students initially make sense of mathematical situations or problems using their own experiences as a frame of reference. As they continue to develop their understanding of numbers, they begin to make purposeful connections to what they know about our base 10 system.

What do you think about the idea of using number-to-self, number-to number, and number-to-world connections to enhance students' awareness and understanding?

Creating mental images is the next comprehension strategy. Students often form a picture in their head while they're reading; similarly, they can build mental models of what is happening within a word problem. Early on, many students use manipulatives or pictures. For example, a young child may be given a problem such as: "I have 4 marbles and Tucker gives me 2 more. How many marbles will I have all together?" He may think about the problem, then represent it by counting out first four, then two more, of his own marbles to help him solve the problem. That is, he will construct a physical picture to correspond to his mental image. Students develop their understanding of operations by recognizing patterns in the way similar problems are solved. Mental images provide a structure and context in which to think about problems, and as students store these images in their mind over time, they are able to move along in their understanding and solve more sophisticated problems.

What are some ways you help your students develop mental pictures when they read? Can you use these same methods to help your students understand math?

Recent research has revealed that *expanding vocabulary* has a major influence on student learning, regardless of which subject is being studied; vocabulary development is as essential in learning to think mathematically as it is in learning to read. It helps students develop their understanding and gives them the ability to articulate what they're learning and thinking in clearer, more concise ways.

Children learn vocabulary primarily indirectly through their conversations with others and the books and programs they're exposed to. However, many words used in mathematics may not come up in everyday contexts—and if they do, they may mean something totally different—so math vocabulary needs to be explicitly taught.

Students construct knowledge as they communicate with each other and work together. Therefore, it is important that students and teachers consistently use accurate math terminology. Explaining words that have different meanings in different contexts is also very important, as students will not automatically know how words they've learned in everyday settings apply to mathematical situations. For example, if a student is asked to determine which of five numbers is the *greatest*, she may choose the one she likes the best as opposed to the largest number. In this example, *greatest* reflects her understanding of a personal preference—her friend Samantha is the greatest friend. Careful attention to helping students differentiate vocabulary is essential for them to accurately communicate their mathematical thinking and understanding.

What are some ways you directly teach your students vocabulary? Can these methods be used in your math class, too?

Asking questions does not refer to something teachers do—here we're not talking about the common practice of clarifying understanding by asking students questions that rely solely on fact recall. Rather, we want to encourage and enable our students to ask questions of themselves while they're working, to clarify their own understanding and to confirm their choice of a method for solving problems—to set up an internal feedback system that helps them use and regulate their mental math capabilities. Most students do not automatically adopt this strategy, so they must be taught to be aware of the power of their thinking as they interact with and communicate about mathematics.

How can you help your students become aware of their own thinking when they're "doing math"?

Learning to understand is an ongoing process that expands across time as students encounter a variety of contexts and purposes for thinking mathematically.

It is important to recognize that students will adapt their strategies to align with their mathematical purpose. Explicit instruction and practice in comprehension strategies early on will enable students to move from less to more sophisticated ways of monitoring their own thinking. Students need to develop strategies of self-awareness that will help them repair their understanding if it is incorrect, incomplete, or lost. The table on page 43 demonstrates the correlation between reading and mathematics thinking processes.

Table 3.2 Properties of Reading and Mathematics

Reading Is Thinking. The mind processes information from many sources at the same time in order to read words and make meaning.	**Mathematics Is Thinking.** The mind processes patterns and relationships in order to explain phenomena or draw logical conclusions.
Reading Is Metacognitive. Readers are aware of their own thinking while reading. They ask questions, make predictions, check for understanding, etc. They self-monitor and adjust.	**Mathematics Is Metacognitive.** Mathematicians are aware of their own thinking. They consider whether a solution makes sense, or whether they have a strategy that will be useful in solving a problem. They self-monitor and adjust.
Reading Is Complex. The process moves from identification of letter sounds to interpretation of printed text.	**Mathematics Is Complex.** Mathematics is a combination of quantitative, logical, and spatial knowledge united by patterns and relationships.
Reading Is Understanding Words and Ideas. Surface and deep structure systems combine to allow for understanding of words and content as readers move through text.	**Mathematics Is Language.** Symbols and specific vocabulary describe mathematical relationships.

Determining importance is crucial for students as they engage in rich mathematical tasks. As younger students develop number sense and begin to combine and compare groups of objects, the amount of unimportant information is pretty minimal. As their number sense develops and math tasks increase in complexity, they learn to recognize information that is not important to the solution of a problem. For example, the following word problem tells us a lot more than we need to know to figure out the answer:

> One Tuesday afternoon on the way home from lacrosse practice, Samantha remembered she had $4.00 to buy a snack. When she came to Eddie's Variety, which was on the way, she picked out a bag of popcorn that cost $1.47 and a green Gatorade that cost

$1.98. She thought about getting a snack for her brother, too. Did she have enough to buy two bags of popcorn?

When students engage in real-world problems, they need to realize what's important (the cost of the items in the above example) before they can arrive at a solution. It's important for students to practice this strategy at an appropriate developmental level—the text should be readable and the numbers not overly complex—so they don't become frustrated and uninterested in developing the strategy.

Determining importance is not the same thing as looking for key words and then applying an operation void of the context. Can you think of ways to give students meaningful practice?

Inferring refers to drawing conclusions from what one reads. Since interacting with text and understanding its relationship to numbers and symbols is a part of numeracy, inferring is an important comprehension strategy for mathematics. Students infer meaning based on their experiences and the nature of the problems presented. Having a variety of experiences to draw from facilitates students' ability to infer in meaningful ways—that is, lots of practice

How do your experiences help you draw conclusions and infer procedures or solutions as you engage in mathematics?

with rich mathematical tasks helps them organize their experiences so that they can draw from them in the future.

Finally, *synthesizing* involves combining new information with existing knowledge to form a new idea or interpretation. Sorting, separating, and evaluating important information can lead to new insights and change the way students think.

The synthesis of ideas can take many forms in the mathematics classroom. Generalizing from observable patterns in numbers, symbols, or shapes; summarizing words, equations, or graphs; applying math concepts to real-life situations; and using deductive reasoning to draw conclusions based on known information are all examples of synthesis. For synthesis to take place, students' experiences and knowledge must be sufficient to allow them to combine ideas in mathematical ways.

What can you synthesize from these seven comprehension strategies?

In summary, understanding can be thought of as the active process of forming mental connections. To understand means to grasp the relationships among mathematical facts, procedures, concepts, and principles by building upon prior knowledge.

The comprehension strategies outlined in the chapter are meant to provide teachers with ways to gauge student understanding and also to show teachers how to give their students meaningful tools to monitor their own learning. If students are to become thoughtful, insightful mathematicians, they must extend their thinking beyond a superficial understanding of numbers and have rich interaction with the mathematics.

As we move to Chapter 4, our focus will shift from defining understanding to determining how students demonstrate their understanding.

4 How Do Students Apply Their Understanding of Numbers?

Being numerate involves having those concepts and skills of mathematics that are required to meet the demands of everyday life. It includes having the capacity to select and use them appropriately in real settings. Being truly numerate requires the knowledge and disposition to think and act mathematically and the confidence and intuition to apply particular mathematical principles to everyday problems.

—*Essential Learnings Framework 1*

This quote speaks of the understanding that underlies mathematical thinking. It suggests being numerate is about having a mathematical sense that enables you to confidently interact with the world in mathematical ways.

The reality is that very few of us, when confronting a situation that requires us to perform division, for instance, take out pencil and paper and begin the long division algorithm. Instead, you probably have some number sense that allows you to engage with the problem without using the "standard" algorithm. You are able to solve the problem based on what you understand about the situation at a conceptual level.

What mathematics do you use in your daily life? What are some of the strategies you use most?

DEVELOPMENTAL OR SEQUENTIAL?

Do you think of mathematics as developmental or sequential in nature? Why?

Mathematics is often referred to as sequential, meaning that students must demonstrate mastery of one idea before they move on to the next. But mathematics is really both sequential and developmental. This idea is important in our consideration of vertical and horizontal curriculum decisions.

Due to the developmental nature of mathematics, some students will grasp the big ideas (concepts) and struggle with the skills that underpin the big ideas. The reverse is also true, as some students will retain facts and demonstrate proficiency with subsets of skills and procedures and have a more difficult time making connections to the big ideas. This is why it is important for us as instructors to understand that providing mathematics in familiar contexts, much as we provide reading in familiar contexts, enables students to use their schema and relate to the mathematics to increase their ability to understand. Students may have some areas of relative strength and others of relative weakness, suggesting that exposure to and practice with all kinds of mathematical ideas are essential.

Given the sequential nature of mathematics, it is equally important that students not be given the message that factual knowledge is somehow the gateway to higher-level mathematics. Often students spend a lot of time memorizing isolated facts and have great difficulty doing so because the facts are not explicitly connected to conceptual understanding. It is as inappropriate to hold a child back from rich mathematics due to incomplete mastery of facts as it would be to hold him or her back from rich text due to lack of spelling ability. Readers are exposed to rich text in order to increase their experiences and support the reading process. Mathematicians need to be exposed to rich, robust mathematics to support their learning as well. Wrapping skills within a context and connecting them to concepts allows students to understand at a deeper, more lasting level.

Sometimes students are excluded from math class because of the "heavy" language usage. If research clearly demonstrates that the early years are the optimal time for learning a foreign language, why would we remove students from the language of mathematics? What do you think?

PROCEDURAL AND CONCEPTUAL UNDERSTANDING

The acquisition of mathematics is embedded in students' ability to reason, solve problems, and articulate their thinking clearly and coherently, and to do so they must rely on both procedural and conceptual knowledge. As mentioned previously, students have the best chance of developing sound mathematical ability when conceptual understanding is emphasized and connected to procedural or factual knowledge. It is in the realization of the relationships and connections between procedures and concepts that true understanding occurs.

> It seems clear that instruction focused solely on symbolic manipulation without understanding is ineffective for most students. It is necessary to correct that imbalance by paying more attention to conceptual understanding as well as the other strands of proficiency and by helping students connect them.
>
> —National Research Council, *Adding It Up*, p. 241

Procedural knowledge refers to the process of systematic manipulation of numbers and symbols following a known rule or pattern.

Procedures include both those that are invented by students and those that are considered conventional or standard. Students need to develop procedural competence based on reasoning in problem-solving situations. This is part of the surface structure of mathematics that we looked at in Chapter 2.

Conceptual understanding forms the deep structure of mathematics and refers to the overarching big ideas that are defined by the patterns in and relationships between skills, procedures, and concepts. Concepts are the forest and procedures, skills, and processes are the trees within the forest. It is difficult for some to see the forest through the trees.

Table 4.1 demonstrates the correlation between the structures of numeracy and the surface and deep structures of reading by giving examples of how surface structures may be compared to procedural knowledge and deep structures to conceptual understanding.

Table 4.1 An Illustration of the Correlation Between the Structures of Numeracy and the Surface and Deep Structures of Reading

Mathematics Strategies and Skills		*Reading Strategies and Skills*	
Procedural	*Conceptual*	*Surface Structure*	*Deep Structure*
Learning the number names in order	Understanding that the number names represent specific quantities	Learning the specific sounds letters make	Developing a sight vocabulary
Learning the standard algorithms for addition and subtraction of whole numbers	Understanding inverse operations and how they are used	Learning sentence structures	Monitoring for meaning if meaning is lost

As you look at Table 4.1, think about how perceiving the correlation between the structures of numeracy and the structures of literacy will affect your instruction. What might procedural knowledge and conceptual understanding look like in the classroom?

In your classroom, do you focus on the trees, the forest, or a combination of both?

> The more mathematical concepts they [students] understand, the more sensible mathematics becomes. In contrast, when students are seldom given challenging mathematical problems to solve, they come to expect that memorizing rather than sense-making paves the road to learning mathematics.
>
> —National Research Council, *Adding It Up*, p. 131

Now that we have looked at procedural knowledge and conceptual understanding, let's take a look at fluency with numbers and at how it relates to understanding. Think about literacy: Even though a student can read words or sentences, this does not necessarily mean he or she understands the text. Being fluent with number words or facts does not always mean students understand numbers.

COMPUTATIONAL FLUENCY WITH WHOLE NUMBERS

In the course of developing number sense, students have opportunities to demonstrate their understanding of our base 10 number system within the context of computation. As they begin to learn basic addition and subtraction in kindergarten, they are building off their understanding of quantity and its relationship to the number names. Students who are ready to compute can count a group of objects and know the total for the group is represented by the last number said—the idea of cardinality. They also develop an understanding of magnitude—the size of objects versus the quantity of objects.

As students' understanding and confidence increase, they extend their number sense to include how numbers are composed and decomposed. This is an important idea, as it is the foundation for part-whole understanding. For example, 5 can be decomposed into 3 and 2 or 4 and 1, and 7 can be composed of 5 and 2 or 4 and 3 or 6 and 1. When students can count quantities comfortably and manipulate them informally by composing and decomposing, they are better prepared to learn the operations of addition and subtraction and understand them at a conceptual level. This is the developmental aspect of numeracy. Students require time and practice to form and solidify a foundation on which to build the sequence.

Fluency with the forward and the backward number sequences and basic number combinations up to 10 provides opportunities for students to see patterns in the base 10 number system and allows for flexibility in strategy development and choice. As students combine small collections of objects using a "count-all" or "count-on" strategy, they are deepening their number knowledge and number sense. Strategy choice is an important clue to how a student is thinking about a situation and what he or she understands or doesn't understand about the numbers and quantities involved in a problem. Asking students to explain what they're doing orally or in writing is a good way of getting them to articulate their thinking. Students can have the right answer for the wrong reason and vice versa; if we focus only on the answer, students' misconceptions and partial understandings will not be revealed. Due to the sequential nature of mathematics, it is imperative to uncover these ideas before they become part of a student's belief system and much more difficult to find and remediate.

Fluency is more than the ability to give rapid-fire responses when asked isolated number facts. While speed is important, it is important only to the extent that it influences strategy choice. The speed with which a reader moves through a passage is only as significant as his or her understanding of what is read.

What is your definition of fluency in reading? In mathematics?

Fluency is the ability to express understanding. It is supported by the development of *efficiency, accuracy*, and *flexibility*. These three ideas help to define what fluency looks like in the classroom.

According to definitions from various sources, fluency is about expression. Take speaking a foreign language, for example: You are considered fluent when you can converse clearly and effortlessly with others. Fluency in mathematics is about expressing mathematical ideas clearly and effortlessly.

To be fluent, students need to be *flexible*—to adapt to new information and be able to choose an effective strategy by adjusting their thinking. Flexibility allows students to demonstrate what they know and understand about a problem based on their having more than one approach to solving it.

> **Please solve the following problem: 1,000**
> **−24**
>
> **What did you do and why? How flexibly did you think about the problem?**
>
> **(Many students will do the subtraction across the zeroes without even considering what the problem is asking. Flexibility allows you to adapt to the numbers used in a particular problem instead of blindly applying a procedure.)**

Efficiency is the ability to apply a strategy to solve a problem without getting lost in the steps. Efficient strategies are developed over time based on experience and derived from a conceptual understanding of the operation. Developing efficiency comes from a personal connection to the mathematics. It is not the result of being shown "the way" but comes from being able to construct one's own understanding in order to refine a given mathematical procedure.

Please solve the following problem in two ways: 27 x 4

How did your second method differ from your first? Which was more efficient? Does one show greater understanding than the other?

(Over time, students move to more sophisticated strategies as they become secure in their understanding of numbers and able to rely on their application of a method or strategy. Efficiency is directly related to a student's current level of understanding of the operation and influenced by the numbers used in the problem.)

Accuracy is still very important in mathematics, despite the "fuzzy math" allegation leveled against the math reform movement. Accuracy is the ability to be precise. Precision comes from recognizing potential errors and achieving accurate results. The correct answer is still a significant part of the mathematical process. Again, you can have the right answer for the wrong reason.

> **Please solve the following problem: 96 students are going on the field trip. I need to order the buses. Each bus can hold 30 students. How many buses do I need to order?**
>
> **How did you think about this problem? Why did you solve it the way you did? Is your answer accurate?**
>
> **(Students who do not consider the nature of the question often will not realize that another bus is required for the "left over" six children. The accuracy is in understanding the question and applying the appropriate mathematical thinking.)**

COMPUTATIONAL STRATEGY CONTINUUMS

The application of numerical understanding is carried out by the development of strategies. The significance of counting cannot be underscored enough in terms of what it means for students developmentally. The strategies students construct in those early years become their foundation on which to balance subsequent skills and concepts.

Students have ideas about numbers prior to formal schooling that influence the way they internalize the role of numbers in their world. Within the literacy research comes a wealth of support for reading to children while they are still in the womb, as this has been linked to strong literacy skills later on. Thus, we read to children before birth and throughout childhood to support their understanding and foster a disposition to think of reading as fun and helpful. To afford them the same benefits when it comes to numbers, it would be beneficial to read them books that have number applications—such as counting—to promote their awareness of numbers in the world. Fostering the use of numbers and mathematics in the everyday lives of children before they start school will better enable them to bring their ideas to the classroom and give them experience upon which to begin building their number knowledge.

When students enter school and begin more formal math instruction, they are introduced to limited or partial concepts about numbers that are appropriate to their developmental level and build as their experience increases. During the early years, PreK through Grade 2, students are exposed to many opportunities to make meaning out of their number knowledge and acquire important strategies and ideas that demonstrate a more thorough conceptual understanding. This pattern continues through the years as they sequentially learn more and more concepts and skills and become more sophisticated mathematical thinkers.

The application of student number knowledge, from understanding place value to working with part-to-whole concepts, is evident within the strategies they choose when computing. The whole decision-making process is very telling. How children represent, articulate, model, and share their thinking is a great window into their level of understanding.

The idea of computational fluency—flexibility, accuracy, and efficiency while computing—is captured in the next four tables. Each operation is placed in a continuum of development to show the progression of strategies. Each relies on a great deal of number sense in order to be effectively used.

The strategies are developmental, and students need much guidance and practice in order to construct them. As they move through the grades, they will move back and forth among these strategies based on the quantities involved and their experience with and understanding of the operation. It is important to remember that when students are asked to demonstrate a strategy for solving a problem,

> Suppose a student solved the following problems like this: 82 – 68 = 26 and 73 – 52 = 21
>
> What would you say this student knows about subtraction? What might you want to ask her?
>
> (Once a student is shown a particular algorithm, he may apply the procedure without considering the reasonableness of his answer rather than invent his own algorithm based on what he currently understands.)

they will do what is most comfortable for them. For example, when your students are learning to count by twos and they are asked to demonstrate this strategy on their own, they will probably resort to counting by ones because this is the strategy they're most familiar and confident with. It is only with enough practice that students develop confidence in using a new or modified strategy accurately and thus begin to choose it more consistently.

Again, it is important to note that students straddle different strategies simultaneously and also move rather flexibly between them. In Chapter 3 we talked about comprehension strategies and vocabulary. Naming strategies by the mathematical ideas embedded within them is an effective way to help students articulate orally and

Count All	Count On	Doubles Plus or Minus	Working With Fives	Making Tens
4 + 3 = Count 4, then count 3, then count all. 1, 2, 3, 4 ○ ○ ○ ○ 1, 2, 3 ○ ○ ○ 1, 2, 3, 4, 5, 6, 7 ○ ○ ○ ○ ○ ○ ○	4 + 3 = 4 + /// = 7 Count or say 4, then continue counting 5, 6, and 7 without going back to 1.	6 + 7 = 6 + 1 **6** + **6** + 1 = 13 (or **7** + **7** – 1 = 13) Doubles are easier facts to recall and can be very useful.	6 + 7 = **5** + 1 + **5** + 2 = 10 + 3 = 13 Decompose numbers to identify fives within numbers and add.	9 + 7 = **9** + 1 6 + **1** **10** + 6 = 16 Identify tens within numbers and add.
Using Compensation	***Using Known Facts***	***Splitting***	***Jumps of 10***	***Next Friendly Number***
8 + 5 = 3 + **2** **8** + 2 **10** + 3 = 13 Compensate by shifting quantities from one addend to the other.	7 + 8 = Think about the numbers and how they may be related. I know that 6 + 8 = 14, so . . . 7 + 8 must be 15.	**2**7 + **4**4 = **20** + 7 **40** + 4 **20** + **40** = 60 7 + 4 = 11 60 + 10 + 1 = 71 This is a landmark strategy using an understanding of place value.	27 + 44 = 44 + 10 + 10 + 7 = 71 **** 348 + 159 = 348 + 100 + 50 + 9 = 507 One number is kept whole and multiples of 10 are added.	98 + 37 = 98 close to 100 100 + 35 = 135 Compensate by shifting quantities to reach a "friendly" number and adjust other addend accordingly.

Points to consider:

- The underlying concept of addition is embedded in counting.
- Students move from counting to combining collections.

Table 4.3 Subtraction Strategies Continuum

Using Counters	*Counting Up*	*Counting Back*	*Making a 10*	*Jumps of 10*	*Using Doubles*	*Related Addition Facts*
8 – 5 = Count out 8 chips and remove 3 chips. 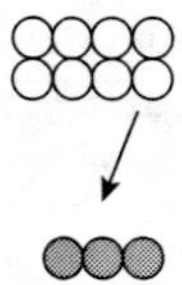 There are 5 chips left. 	8 – 5 = 5, 6, 7, 8 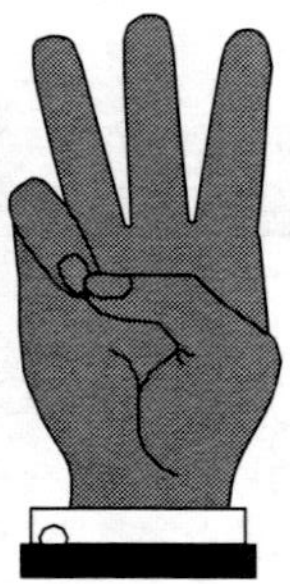	9 – 2 = 9, 8, 7 9 in your head, count back	Knowing 6 + 4 = 10 can be helpful in finding differences from 10 . . . 10 – 6 = 4 and 10 – 4 = 6 May be used to reinforce close facts: 9 – 4 = 5 11 – 4 = 7	Using a pattern of jumps of 10 . . . 17 – 10 = 7 13 – 10 = 3 . . . may be used to reinforce close facts: 17 – 9 will be 1 more than 17 – 10.	Knowing 8 + 8 = 16 and 6 + 6 = 12 Uses the idea of "half doubles": 16 – 8 = 8 12 – 6 = 6 May be used to reinforce close facts: 15 – 8 = 7 13 – 6 = 7	Use reasoning to draw from known facts. Knowing that 8 + 7 = 15 is helpful in solving 15 – 7 = 8. Seeing relationships between operations is vital for fluency and flexibility.

Points to consider:

- Subtraction and addition are inherently connected, so strategies are similar.
- An understanding of the relationship between addition and subtraction needs to be developed within contexts first.
- "Adding on" versus "removing" is a central idea in subtraction; it is important to know when to use which strategy. When numbers are closer together, it is easier to add on; when they are farther apart, it is easier to work backward.
- Students need to use and understand a variety of vocabulary that describes subtraction. "Take away" implies a strategy, and if it is the only vocabulary used, it determines the strategy. Other vocabulary words that can be used include difference, subtract, and remove.
- Compensation is a common strategy for addition, and many students will generalize this idea and apply it to subtraction. However, it does not work for subtraction. Subtraction requires that a "constant difference" remain.
- Students use many models to show their thinking. Models may include number lines, splitting, swapping, friendly numbers, canceling out common amounts, etc. All are ways to demonstrate understanding.

Table 4.4 Multiplication Strategies Continuum

Representing Each Item Counting by Ones	*Repeated Addition (Skip Counting)*	*Unitizing (Counting By)*	*Doubling*	*Halving and Doubling*
How many crackers are there total in 3 bags containing 4 crackers each? Count each group separately, then count the whole. ○○○○ ○○○○ ○○○○	How many crackers are there total in 3 bags containing 4 crackers each? Count by saying $4+4=8$ and $8+4=12$ or by saying 4,8,12. ○○○ ○○○ ○○○ ○○○	How many toy cars are there total in5 boxes containing 7 cars each? 5 + 2 5 + 2 5 + 2 5 + 2 5 + 2 Five 5s and five 2s: 5,10, 15, 20,25, plus 2×5,which equals 10. $25+10=35$	$2\times3\times6=$ 6×6 Recognize that 2×3 is a double of 3, which is 6. Supports flexibility with number sense.	$4\times3=2\times6$ Split the 4 in half and double the 3. Supports flexibility with number sense.

Using the Distributive Property	*Using the Distributive Property with Tens*	*Using the Commutative Property*	*Associative Property*
9×6 $(5\times6)+(4\times6)$ 12×11 $(6\times11)+(6\times11)$ or $(12\times12)-12$	9×8 $(10\times8)-8$ 23×19 $(23\times20)-23$	$6\times7=7\times6$ $28\times5=5\times28$ $30\times12=12\times30$	$(7\times5)\times3=7\times(5\times3)$ (The order in which the factors are multiplied does not affect the answer.)

Points to consider:

- Skip counting is helpful in learning multiplication facts, as is the array model.
- Students should be exposed to many different types of problems and situations involving multiplication.
- Repeated addition is an effective model for multiplication of whole numbers.
- Multiplication does not always result in a larger product.
- Multiplication and division are inverse operations.

Table 4.5 Division Strategies Continuum

Representing Each Group and Counting All (Quotative Situation)	*Repeated Addition, Skip Counting, Counting On (Quotative Situation)*	*Using the Distributive Property of Multiplication (Quotative Situation)*	*Using the Commutative Property of Multiplication (Paritive Situation)*
How many tables will we need for 36 people if we seat 4 people at each table?	How many tables will we need for 36 people if we seat 4 people at each table?	How many tables will we need for 36 people if we seat 4 people at each table?	If there are 36 people to seat at 9 tables, how many can sit at each table?
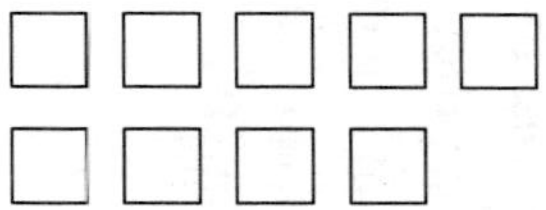 1, 2, 3, 4, 5, 6, 7 . . . 36	4 4 4 4, 8, 12, 16 . . . 36	$5 \times 4 = 20$ $4 \times 4 = 16$ $\textcircled{9} \times 4 = 36$	Count out 36 cubes and put them one by one into 9 groups. Stop when all cubes are distributed and count the number of cubes in one of the groups.
Make representations of the tables and add 4 tallies for each table, then count tallies up to 36. Now go back and count the number of tables the 36 tallies occupy.	Make representations of the tables and put a 4 on each table. Count by 4s to 36 and determine the number of tables by the number of 4s said.	Use simpler multiplication facts to determine the number of 4s needed to reach 36 (9 tables needed).	This strategy and paritive situation relies on a student's knowledge of fair shares and equal groups.

Points to consider:

- Division is more than repeated subtraction or the opposite of multiplication.
- There are two types of division contexts students need to be exposed to: quotative and paritive. Each kind of problem is solved using a different strategy.
- Quotative situations ask how many groups there are when the size of the group is known.
- Paritive situations ask how many are in the group when the number of groups is known.
- Division is central to working with fractions, percents, and proportions.
- Knowing multiplication facts and understanding multiplicative situations is essential to success in division.

in writing what they did. Writing in math class should be of a technical nature rather than a creative one. Therefore, providing students with examples of what a specific strategy (such as "counting on") looks like helps them to recognize it for themselves when they do it.

Do these continuums make sense as a way to help your students identify the mathematics in their strategies? How can these continuums affect your instruction?

In this chapter we looked at the developmental and sequential nature of mathematics, the role of procedural and conceptual understanding, and the application of understanding through computation.

Our goal is to help our students express their numeracy with the same degree of confidence with which they express their literacy. Table 4.6 summarizes the overarching behaviors of effective readers and mathematicians. This comparison can help teachers grasp what it means to be effective and define the behaviors that support success in mathematics.

Table 4.6 Behaviors of Effective Readers and Mathematicians

Effective readers think *within the text.* Example: Students pick up basic information to understand what the text is about.	Effective mathematicians think *within the numbers/problem.* Example: Students determine the basic relationship within a problem to understand what is being asked.
Effective readers think *beyond the text.* Example: Students draw on their own knowledge and experience to make sense of what they are reading.	Effective mathematicians think *beyond the numbers/problem.* Example: Students draw on their own knowledge and experience to make sense of the numbers and problems they are presented with.
Effective readers think *about the text.* Example: Students step back from the text to notice how it is written, understand the language, admire the writing, or critique the writing.	Effective mathematicians think *about the numbers/problem.* Example: Students step back from the problem to notice how it is written, understand the language, notice the relationships, or form conjectures.

The following chapter provides opportunities to consider instructional strategies for use in the mathematics classroom and gives examples of how other teachers have made sense of the ideas presented in this book in their classrooms.

5 How Do Teachers Connect Ideas to Practice?

You may initially plan the whole journey or only part of it. You set out sailing according to your plan. However, you must constantly adjust because of the conditions that you encounter. You continue to acquire knowledge about sailing, about the current conditions, and about the areas that you wish to visit. You change your plans with respect to the order of your destinations. You modify the length and nature of your visits as a result of interactions with people along the way. You add destinations that prior to the trip were unknown to you. The path that you travel is your [actual] trajectory. The path that you anticipate at any point is your "hypothetical trajectory."

—Martin Simon, "Reconstructing Mathematics Pedagogy From a Constructivist Perspective," pp. 136–137

As the quote above suggests, it is essential that we continue to address the challenges we face in our mathematics classrooms today. We must give numeracy the same due diligence we have given literacy in order to support the time and resources change will require. It is not enough to identify the problem; we must also acknowledge the trajectory, or course, we're taking, build capacity for a shared purpose, and set in motion opportunities to plan the journey together.

This book is all about demonstrating the connections between literacy instruction and numeracy instruction. My belief is that we can capitalize on what have been identified as effective practices for teaching literacy and parallel them to practices for teaching numeracy. This is not to say that there are no significant differences within the content areas themselves, but identifying similarities is a place for educators to start conversations that will build capacity for more meaningful dialogue and progress.

In this chapter, I will pass along anecdotes and ideas that other teachers have shared with me and also explain more specifically some of the instructional strategies I've referred to throughout the book.

INSTRUCTIONAL STRATEGIES

The ideas, activities, and strategies presented in this chapter are for use in math classrooms, and are derived from practices effectively used to teach reading and other subjects. My purpose is to help you begin to see "math class" more like a workshop—a place where students engage in similar mathematical activities (guided instruction, individual and group work, practice, discussion, and sharing) within a classroom structure. Rather than taking a traditional lock-step approach that moves all students in a similar direction in the same way regardless of their understanding, teachers can model the structure of a reading and writing workshop and utilize the same processes in order to meet a variety of students' needs.

In providing examples of what I have done in my own classroom and observed in my colleagues' classrooms, my intent is to set your own creative energy free. My aim is to lighten your load, not increase it.

Teacher Talk along the way will allow you to see how other teachers have made sense of these connections and are using the strategies and ideas in their classrooms to enrich the teaching and learning of mathematics. Questions throughout the chapter give you opportunities to make connections to your current practice.

WORD WALLS

Do you currently or have you ever used a "word wall" in your classroom? Why did you use it? How did your students respond?

Word walls are not a new idea—they support vocabulary development and spelling ability. But their use is typically limited to helping students learn to read and write.

In previous chapters, we have discussed the importance of vocabulary development. Building vocabulary is fundamental to overall comprehension of any subject matter, and mathematics is no exception. Mathematics is a language of its own, and students need explicit demonstration of, practice with, and application of vocabulary in order to truly make sense of their thinking and work. Word walls are a great way to support language acquisition, as they can include symbols and pictures to further enhance language development and solidify understanding.

Teacher Talk

As a second grade teacher, I began to notice that the vocabulary my students were using to describe their mathematical understanding was fairly generic and not very accurate. They used "plussed" and "take away" a great deal, both orally and in writing. It seemed to me that in order for me to expect them to use the appropriate labels for operations as well as have more than one way to talk about their thinking, I needed to not only provide them with

(Continued)

(Continued)

the words in my instruction, but also create a place for them to refer to as they did their work.

I started small by creating a wall space next to our Reading Wall entitled Math Wall. As we debriefed the daily activities, I would ask for words to add to the math wall. When a word was offered, we discussed it as a group to build a common definition and posted that definition with the word. Also, students would provide examples from their work to show what the word looked like "in action." As the year and student experiences grew, so did our math wall. Many words were moved around as students began connecting them by similarities and differences. They used the language from reading and writing class to classify words as antonyms and synonyms, too. This not only provided the enrichment for math vocabulary, but also gave me more data about what they really understood from our language arts work.

—A second-grade teacher

Teachers do need to be purposeful in their interaction with the word wall, both in what is added and in how specific words are to be used within the classroom. For example, within a literacy classroom, it is common to clearly represent the "nonnegotiable" spelling words of a particular grade on the word wall for students to use as a resource when they are writing. In a mathematics classroom, that same word wall could include the names of the "big ideas" that are emerging from student experiences. Those ideas could then be grouped together in such a way as to show the connections between them—for example, addition and subtraction as inverse operations. Long before students name the *inverse relationship*, they are playing with the underlying definition of that idea.

Figure 5.1 is an example of a growing word wall.

VOCABULARY ENHANCEMENT IDEAS

According to a meta-analysis conducted by McREL (Marzano, Pickering, & Pollock, 2001), nine types of instructional strategies have been demonstrated to increase achievement for all students across all grades and all subjects. Vocabulary development, through direct instruction of words that are critical to new content, produces the most benefit to learners. Students require experience with

Figure 5.1 Third-Grade Word Wall

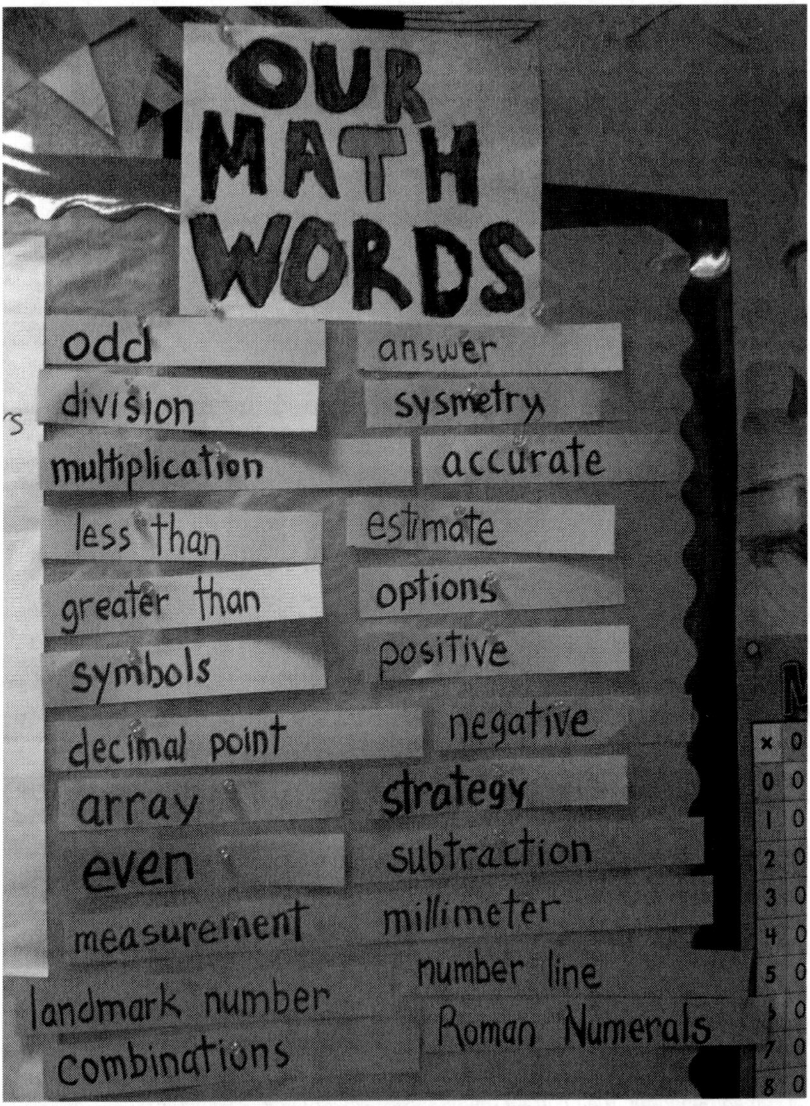

the vocabulary they encounter in text before they can make meaning of what they read. Similarly, they need instruction in mathematics vocabulary to support their understanding of math text.

What do you do to support your math students' vocabulary development?

In literacy class, students are immersed in language. Removing struggling readers from rich language experiences is not considered appropriate, as it would deprive them of the opportunity to hear, see, say, and write words. Teachers can reinforce vocabulary for students by creating both language-rich and print-rich environments. Because the specialized vocabulary of math is rarely if ever heard on the playground or at home, immersion in school is necessary. For example, what do the following words mean to you: *radical, decompose, factor*? How about *add* and *compose*? In helping students use vocabulary accurately, teachers have an important way to assess student understanding.

Teacher Talk

In my fourth-grade classroom, I decided to create an interactive bulletin board focused on mathematics vocabulary in order to make the language explicit and connected for my students. The idea was to take a concept, topic, or big idea that we were going to work on and create a vocabulary web that grew as our knowledge grew.

For example, when we began the unit on algebra, I drew a large oval containing the word Algebra *in big letters in the center of the bulletin board. Students then generated their current definitions of algebra, and we charted them and also added some words to our web. As the unit unfolded, students continued to add vocabulary with supporting definitions and examples related to algebra and made connections in their written and oral explanations. At the end of the unit, we referred back to the definitions and understandings we had charted at the beginning of the unit and compared them to our current level of understanding. Students communicated with such confidence and accuracy about what they understood from the unit. The experience was invaluable.*

—A fourth-grade teacher

Figure 5.2 Fourth-Grade Bulletin Board

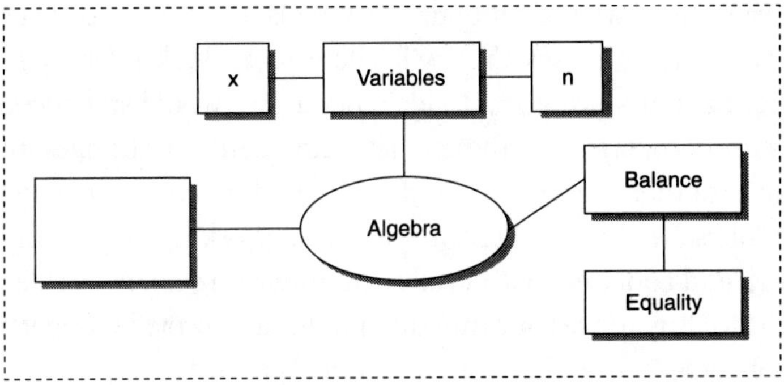

All support materials do not need to be created, as many commercially made games can be modified to support mathematics vocabulary development and most mathematics programs come with support materials to help students in the acquisition of math vocabulary. There are online supports as well, from interactive programs designed for students to sites that help teachers create materials to use in their classrooms. It's important to choose developmentally appropriate materials that line up with your unit and lesson objectives.

Here are some examples of games and activities that support vocabulary development:

? Concentration
? Word bingo
? Scattegories
? Scrabble
? Crossword puzzles

Can you think of other games or activities that could be adapted to support mathematics vocabulary development?

CREATIVE VERSUS TECHNICAL WRITING

One reason we write down our thinking is to create a "hard copy" of our thought processes that will allow us to look back at how we thought about a problem, decide whether we would still document it the same way, and determine what refinements or changes might be made. Another reason is that in mathematics, communication with both ourselves and others is essential. Working to communicate clearly and concisely both orally and in writing helps us solidify our own thinking, makes our thinking public, and provides opportunities for conversations within a mathematical context.

Figure 5.3 Second-Grade Student Work

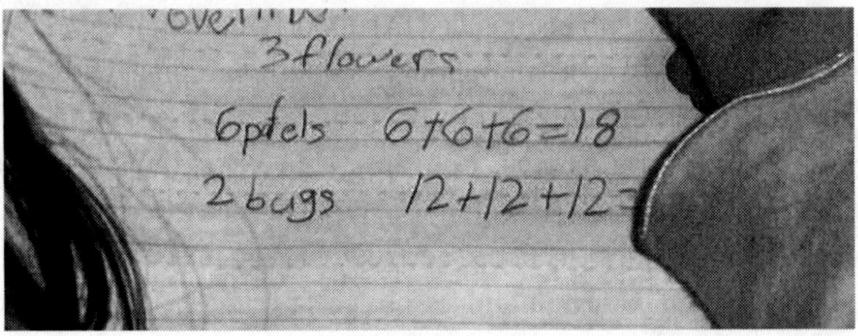

From our study of language development, we know that a word needs to be used at least seven times before it becomes part of a student's vocabulary. To effectively communicate their understanding in writing, students need to know the vocabulary of the subject they're dealing with. Therefore, it is crucial that we expose students to the specific mathematical vocabulary that is developmentally appropriate for them. The word walls and interactive bulletin boards mentioned previously support students as they write by serving as a reference point.

Writing in math is *technical writing*. It is not flowery or fanciful, but clear, concise, and accurate. It is not always in words, as the symbols of the language are just as important and can sometimes communicate even more clearly and effectively. To support our students' language acquisition and strategy development, we should encourage them to use pictures, words, and symbols to communicate their thinking.

The following figure demonstrates the range of ways a group of first-grade students thought about solving problems. Some drew the objects to represent the quantities or numbers involved, another used a number line, and still another used the strategy of splitting. All are appropriate, and all are evidence of student understanding.

Figure 5.4 First-Grade Sample of Written Work

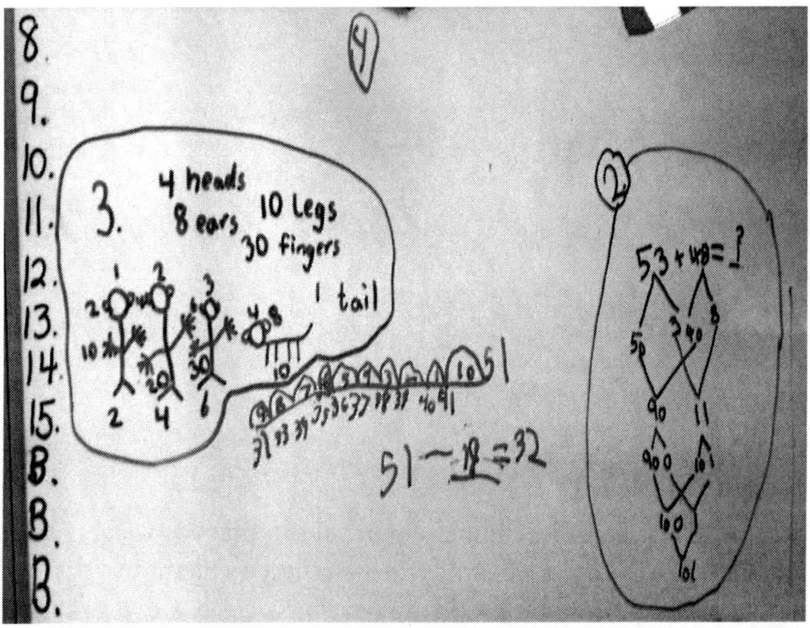

An important point to remember is that quite often students who consider writing laborious will do less mathematically if they think they have to write everything down just as they did it. This is why it is important to differentiate between types of writing, considering both purpose and audience. A student's writing ability should be separate from what he or she understands and can demonstrate mathematically. The figures in Chapter 2 illustrate how students initially regard correct spelling and sentence structure necessary for sharing mathematical thinking. The need to use perfect words influences students to choose the easiest-to-describe method rather than more sophisticated strategies or ideas.

Have you previously thought about the creative versus technical aspects of writing as they relate to your students? Can you see how modifying your expectations for your students' communication could positively affect how they express themselves mathematically?

MATH JOURNALS

Capturing student thinking in a journal is a practice widely used in literacy development; students write to reflect on literature they read, write to practice writing, write to develop a voice, etc. Journals are very flexible; they can be directed by the teacher to reflect desired results of instruction, or they can be more free flowing to allow for independent use. Regardless of the purpose, the journal becomes documentation of thoughts or growth over time. Given that mathematics is developmental, sequential, and a language of its own, a math journal is an instructional tool teachers to help children monitor their own thinking and document their own growth to support metacognition.

Have you used journaling with your students for mathematics? If not, how might you guide them to use a journal?

What might a journal add as evidence of student learning in mathematics?

Teacher Talk

In my first-grade classroom, I make math journals for my students to work on as they wait for me to get ready for the day. The journals give the children extra practice solving problems and opportunities to explain their thinking outside our math block. They also give me evidence of how my students are doing.

I generally create a journal each week. giving my students time to solve problems. I ask them to show a picture solution, create a number sentence, and explain their thinking in words, giving them a chance to build their strategy repertoire. There isn't a great deal of space to write, so students practice being specific.

Each week we share problems from the math journals and students share their strategies for the class to see. This is another opportunity for students to practice using the language of mathematics.

I find that my first-graders develop great skill by the end of the school year and feel confident in their ability to communicate their thinking.

—A first-grade teacher

Mathematics journals can be used in a variety of ways, depending on the age of the students and the purpose of the journal. Students can work on specific kinds of problems, build their strategies, make connections to the real world, and write about their thinking to build a collection of evidence that documents their learning.

Using journals as a place for reflection can be very powerful in mathematics. Reflecting on an activity or process enables students to further refine their understanding. Open-ended questions can be used to solicit that thinking. Here are some examples of questions you might use in your math class that are commonly used in language arts classes:

1. What did you notice?
2. What surprised you?
3. Did you find any patterns?
4. Why do you think it worked the way it did?
5. Can you make any connections?

Questions like these, when used occasionally, allow students to be more thoughtful about their thinking and more purposeful in their communication of ideas.

Figure 5.5 is an example of a journal page from a first-grade classroom. The teacher had created a problem for the day and asked the students to solve it and write about their thinking.

For older students, a math journal can be used to extend student thinking and create evidence for them to use during conferences to share their growth. Figure 5.6 shows how one teacher created a template that focused her students' attention on what she wanted them to work on. Students completed these reflections weekly and kept them in their math binder.

Figure 5.5 First-Grade Math Journal Sample

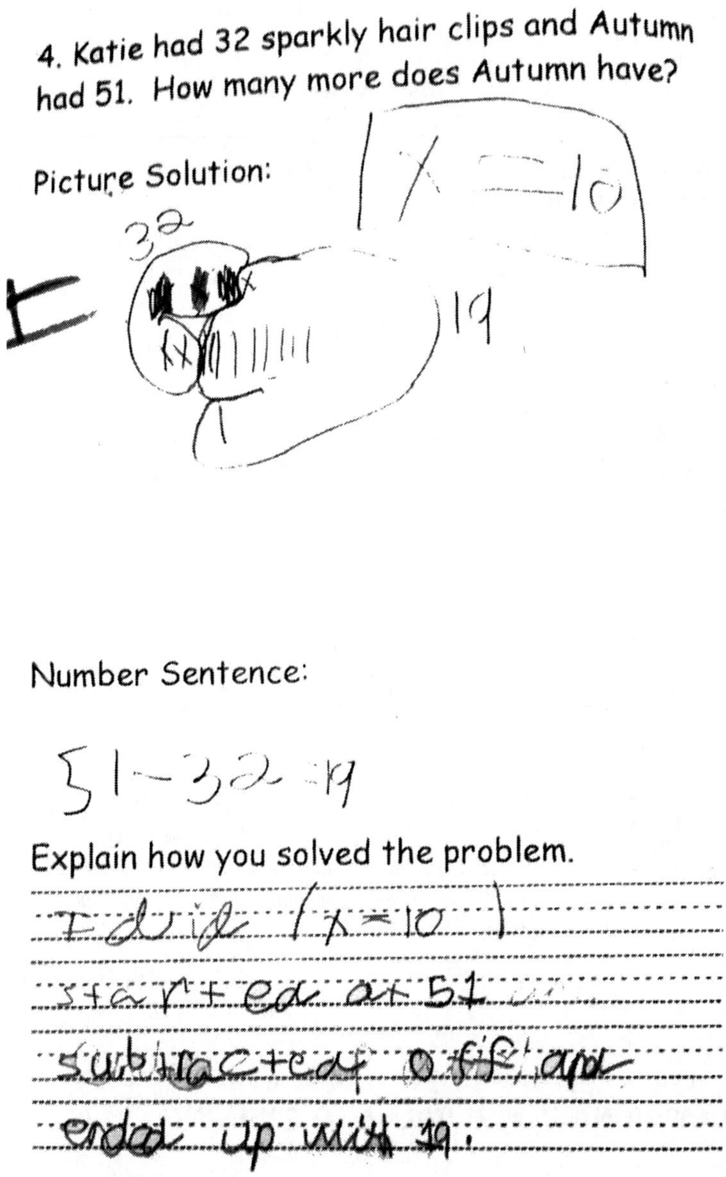

4. Katie had 32 sparkly hair clips and Autumn had 51. How many more does Autumn have?

Picture Solution:

Number Sentence:

51 − 32 = 19

Explain how you solved the problem.

I did (X = 10) started at 51 subtracted off, and ended up with 19.

Figure 5.6 A Math Journal Idea

Name: Date:

Math Reflection

What "math" did you use to solve the problem?	How did you know to use it?
Did this problem make you think of a similar problem?	How could you add to this problem to make it a little more challenging?

Teacher Talk

Place value is all about identifying individual digits in a number. This is similar to identifying the individual sounds in a word as you sound out words. You can pull numbers apart by their place value and pull words apart by their individual letters.

—A first-grade teacher

COMPARING PLACE VALUE TO SPELLING

In elementary schools, spelling skills get a lot of instructional time. Students focus on spelling both in class and when they do their homework. They work on it in writing class and in reading class, and quite often spelling is a subject of its own.

For me, thinking about how to spell is similar to thinking about place value and how to build "number words."

If building words is putting together isolated sounds to create a combination with its own meaning, then what is putting together isolated digits to create a number with its own quantity? If words have different purposes and can be used in a variety of ways, do numbers have different purposes also? If sentences are created to add more depth and information to words, will adding symbols and operations add more depth and information to numbers? Some words change their meaning when they are combined with other words. Do numbers change their meaning, or their value, when they are combined with other numbers?

The parallel for me is in thinking about the single digit. While the English alphabet consists of 26 distinct letters, in mathematics we have 10 single digits, 0 through 9. From these basic symbols in our mathematics "alphabet" come an infinite number of transformations that communicate the language of mathematics. Digits are put together to spell "math words."

What do you think of the "math alphabet" idea? Does it make you think of the strategies you use to teach spelling?

Teacher Talk

I see a connection between literacy and numeracy. For instance, students use "chunking" to compose words. They think about the chunks that make up words as they build them and take them apart. To build the word **find**, *a student would choose the tile* **ind** *first and then add* **f**. *To build the number 37, a student would think of the 30 first and then the 7. In both contexts, students seem to build their understanding by chunking pieces to create the whole.*

—*A second-grade teacher*

Students can benefit from being given many opportunities to put numbers together and take them apart. When students have an understanding of how our base 10 number system is designed, they can think flexibly about numbers and apply a variety of strategies to solve problems. The number wheel is one structure that helps students develop their understanding by allowing them to choose a number to work with and respond to questions related to facts about that number. By changing the questions asked or numbers used, teachers can present a great variety of number ideas.

Figure 5.7 Number Wheel

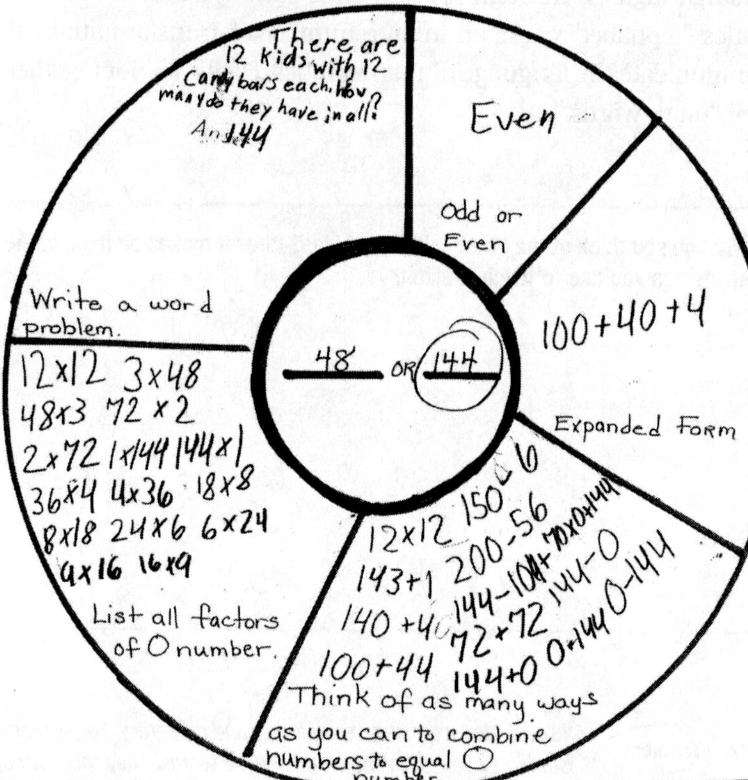

MANIPULATIVES

Young students rely on pictures, puppets, and other tangible objects to help them interpret a story they have heard or read. These props, or manipulatives, allow them to engage with the characters and build the story. And so it is for students and math. Manipulatives help move students from a concrete understanding to a more abstract understanding. As students progress in their experiences with and understanding of number, the kinds of manipulatives they use may change with the concepts they're learning, but the support they offer to the construction of ideas remains the same.

Students can begin to grasp ideas about place value through the use of manipulatives. But the key to unlocking manipulatives' potential is in realizing that their use does not guarantee student understanding. It would be naive to believe that the move from handling or perceiving objects to comprehending mathematical abstraction is automatic. Thoughtful instruction on the purpose of using the manipulatives is necessary, as not all manipulatives are conducive to all math thinking. Certain manipulatives offer students an opportunity to view or perform actions from which concepts may be abstracted. The abstractions are not always easily made, and therefore much practice is necessary. Students build their understanding over time.

How do you help your students move from the concrete to the abstract? Do you use manipulatives to help them build understanding?

STRATEGY DEVELOPMENT

In transitioning from the use of manipulatives to the abstraction of concepts comes the development of strategies. The computation continuums in Chapter 4 provide students and teachers with the mathematical ideas underlying the strategies as well as the names of the strategies. When students state that they used *compensation* to add two numbers, they are using very clear and concise language to convey their thinking. The continuums can also help teachers assist their students in developing multiple strategies for computing based on their knowing how their students are thinking about particular problems.

Teacher Talk

As part of the work my district did with Leslie, our entire group of PreK–5 teachers, including special education teachers, was introduced to the computation continuums.

I have taught as an elementary teacher at different levels for many, many years. For the first time, I was able to get a better sense of what my students were doing with computation and how I might help them move their thinking and understanding. It was helpful to finally have a way to know what the next step might be. I know that students don't move in a linear fashion necessarily, but by choosing the numbers in problems and being specific about the strategies shared by students, I was able to help students develop multiple strategies to solve problems.

I also wanted my students to work with the continuums and take some responsibility for their own learning. I made a chart for each of the strategies for the addition continuum and posted the charts on the bulletin board. Then I had students post their solutions to problems underneath the strategy they used. This provided students with both a model of what the strategy was called and also a model of what it looked like to use the strategy. Students used the strategy names to write about their mathematics thinking. For example, in describing how they solved 15 + 23, students would normally say, "I added the 5 + 3 and got 8 and put that down then I added the 1 and the 2 and got 3 and put that down and wrote 38." But now students could say, and I expected them to say, "I used splitting this time by keeping the 10 and 20 whole and got 30. I knew that 5 + 3 was 8, added 30 + 8 and got 38."

A benefit of posting the strategies and having students interact with them in meaningful ways was that their mathematical language grew exponentially. They were confident in explaining themselves because they were using the "real" math words, as one of my students told me. Another benefit to using the computation continuums was that they gave students and teachers in our schools shared expectations and vocabulary. This has had a huge impact on our grade level and vertical team math conversations.

—An elementary school teacher

The two student samples on page 86 illustrate the distinction between what I, as a teacher, see as different degrees of student understanding. The fact that a student refers to a number in the tens place as a single digit shows that he or she does not necessarily understand place value. When computing, many students will apply a procedure without considering first what they understand about the numbers involved in the problem or the relationship of the numbers to each other.

The Student A work sample shows a student's ability to be accurate and demonstrate the standard algorithm for double-digit addition. The question would be whether or not this student's work demonstrates an understanding of place value.

Figure 5.8 Student A Work Sample

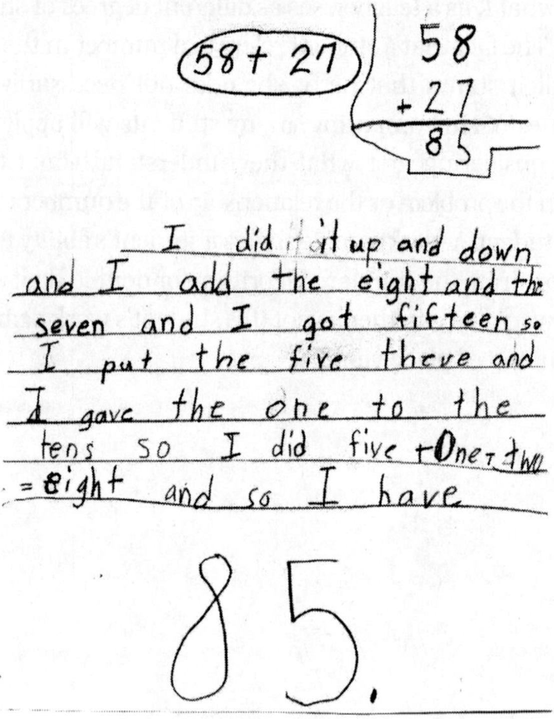

Figure 5.9 Student B Work Sample

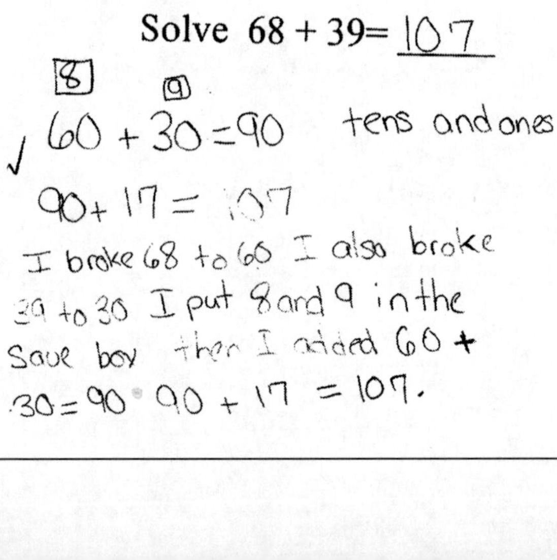

Look at Student A's work sample. What do you see as evidence of this student's understanding of place value? (Be specific.)

Now look at Student B's work sample. What do you see as evidence of this student's understanding of place value? (Be specific.)

Can you see a difference in the level of understanding shared by each student? Is it easy to interpret their thinking?

Would you want to ask the first student a clarifying question? What might you ask?

The Student B sample provides clearer evidence that the student looked at the numbers in the problem and decided on a strategy based on the numbers. When students have multiple strategies to choose from as they engage in problems, they are able to make decisions based on multiple factors. If they have only one strategy, they are likely to use it without considering the numbers in the problem or the context. This has been demonstrated by a project I am involved in called Early Mathematical Thinking, currently being piloted by 25 school sites across Maine and funded by the Maine Department of Education. As part of this project, diagnostic interview tools are used to screen students as they enter a grade and give teachers relevant information regarding their number knowledge. The following example clearly illustrates how students may rely too heavily on a procedure without considering what they know about the numbers involved in the problem. During the screening, students are be shown a card with $25 + 99$ on it and asked to solve it. Most third- and fourth-graders will look at the problem, write 25 under the 99, and begin adding. While they may produce the correct response (124), their true level of conceptual understanding remains unclear. Blindly applying a procedure without thinking about the numbers is a little akin to reading words correctly at an adequate speed without being able to retell what has been read.

How does this example resonate with your experiences with your students? Do you have students who respond very procedurally to problems?

How could you help students recognize the importance of considering the numbers and the context (if there is one) when they solve problems?

THE GRAND FINALE

The one word all educators would like to have removed from current conversations might be *assessment*. As a nation, we are certainly experiencing much turmoil and anxiety when it comes to assessing students in reading and math. I believe that NCLB's silver lining will appear when we put time, money, and resources into our schools to support our teachers in becoming more articulate and knowledgeable about what matters in mathematics. If we are to impact pedagogy in a meaningful way, assessment of student knowledge must be part of the conversation.

FORMATIVE ASSESSMENT

In this age of assessment, it is essential to understand the roles of formative and summative assessment in instruction. Much current research offers educators the opportunity to think about the distinction between assessment *for* learning and assessment *of* learning. The distinction is very important to make, as mathematical assessment has historically been an assessment *of* learning. Tests and quizzes have determined student aptitude and achievement, and grade point averages have decided which math track students pursue. Assessment *of* learning is evaluative and therefore serves a purpose. However, there is another kind of assessment.

Formative assessment—as opposed to summative assessment—informs instruction. The goal of formative assessment is to determine students' prior knowledge and use the information to drive instruction. To use formative assessment, teachers must feel comfortable identifying what their students need to know and recognizing what it looks like when their students demonstrate that understanding. It is essential to realize which big ideas and central themes students must comprehend to become numerate.

Uncovering Student Thinking in Mathematics (Rose, Minton, & Arline, 2006) is a resource two of my colleagues and I developed to support teachers in using research-based diagnostic probes to access students' prior knowledge and uncover any misconceptions or misunderstandings they may have. This book, while providing the 25 formative assessment probes, also provides teachers with a process to create their own formative assessment probes for use in their own classroom.

Do you currently have formative assessment strategies that you find useful in math class? If not, are there strategies that you use to teach literacy that you might consider using in math class?

QUESTIONS TO INFORM INSTRUCTION

Questioning and observation are examples of instructional strategies educators can incorporate to gain insight into student understanding. These instructional strategies become formative assessment if the results are used to design activities to address the specific needs of the students as they relate to a specific learning target.

Good questions and observations allow the math instructor to gather information about a single student or classroom of students in order to inform his or her instruction. It is important to know which questions are likely to elicit the kind of information that will be helpful. Table 5.1 offers questions to consider when observing students engaged in mathematics tasks, activities, or games. Gathering responses to a few of these questions can be very helpful in planning next steps. Observing students allows you to see and hear them as they work to construct their own meaning, giving you a view different from the one paper and pencil supplies.

Table 5.1 Questions to Consider

How do students approach the problem? Do they seem to understand the problem and begin to solve it, or are they uncertain of how to begin?	Do students come up with their own strategies or do they let others tell them what to do? What do their strategies reveal about their level of understanding?
Do students solve the problem fluently using mathematical reasoning, and can they communicate it effectively?	Do students understand that there is more than one strategy for solving problems? Do they communicate their strategies and try to understand others?
How effectively do students use materials/manipulatives to help them with their mathematical work?	Do students have organized ways for keeping track of and recording their work?

What kinds of questions do you ask to determine whether or not a student understands the mathematics?

SELF-ASSESSMENT TO INFORM INSTRUCTION

Student self-assessment is another instructional strategy that allows teachers to get a sense of how students are thinking about math ideas. As students develop the vocabulary of mathematics and practice technical writing, they become quite adept at articulating their progress against a learning target.

Developing criteria with your students to help them become more involved in and more responsible for their own learning is incredibly invaluable to them, as they develop a very clear understanding of what the expectations for success are and become able to monitor and assess the quality of their work for themselves. Figure 5.10 is an example of a self-assessment rubric used to help third-graders take on the responsibility of evaluating their own work against defined criteria. The teacher in this class decided that he wanted to focus on three areas with his students: communication, accuracy, and reasoning. He then built the rubric to show stages of quality for each of these areas. Students used the rubric to make decisions about their own work. The teacher evaluated the student's work using an identical copy, and when there were differences of opinion, the two would conference to talk about the work sample and come to a shared opinion based on the evidence provided by the work.

Figure 5.10 Math Self-Assessment Rubric

Your Keys to Math Success. . . .

Driver: Date:

C Communication	Clear and Complete Communication of Thinking	Clear but Incomplete Communication of Thinking	Unclear and Incomplete Communication of Thinking
A Accuracy	Answers Are Accurate (Correct)	Answers Are Inaccurate but Reasonable	Answers Are Inaccurate and Not Reasonable
R Reasoning	Strategies Are Effective and Efficient	Strategies Are Effective	Strategies Are Ineffective

Figure 5.11 gives examples of self-assessment response cards students completed and attached to their portfolio work in preparation for student-led conferences. This kind of self-assessment is very powerful for students. Parents are often very impressed with how their children communicate their mathematical understanding, including their knowledge of their strengths and areas they need to work on.

Figure 5.11 Self-Assessment Response Cards

This is an example of:
understanding division

The evidence of this is:
Journal page 17
Student Sheet 20
Homework 3/18

Name: JanWillem
Date: 5/11/03

I have collected the following samples of work:
Student Sheet 8
Score sheet to close to 100
Math Think Sheet - subtraction

They are evidence of my growth in:
Math

The growth is:
I can now explain how to solve subtraction problems accurately with words and an algorithm.

Please Notice:

? I have used math vocabulary words correctly to explain my thinking.

? I used 2 different strategies to solve the multiplication problem.

Name: Tucker
Date: 11/23/03

I used to:
not be able to explain how I got my answers

And now I:
Slow down and think about what to write so people can understand what I am trying to say

Name: Samantha
Date: April 19, 2003

How do you help your students talk about themselves as mathematicians?

THE REAL GRAND FINALE

The purpose of this book has been to bring about an awareness of the similarities between literacy and numeracy and also to share the experiences of teachers who have benefited from adapting their literacy instructional strategies to support numeracy instruction.

In *Holding Sacred Ground* (2003), Carl Glickman shares research on teacher cognition, specifically disclosing how teachers take in new information regarding their practice. He notes: "Piaget viewed assimilation and accommodation as the twin processes of cognition. You must have some familiarity with a new idea to process it (assimilation), but then, as you process the idea, your mental organization changes to incorporate the new idea into a larger concept (accommodation)" (p. 129).

It is my hope that the information presented in this book did build on what you know (assimilation), and that as you think about the ideas we have discussed, you will indeed incorporate what makes sense to you into your own practice (accommodation).

References

Ashlock, R. B. (2002). *Error patterns in computation: Using error patterns to improve instruction* (8th ed.). Englewood Cliffs, NJ: Prentice Hall.

Ball, D. L. (2003). *What mathematical knowledge is needed for teaching mathematics?* Remarks prepared for Secretary's Summit on Mathematics, U.S. Department of Education.

Barth, R. S. (2001). *Learning by heart.* San Francisco: Jossey-Bass.

Barth, R. S. (2003). *Lessons learned.* Thousand Oaks, CA: Corwin Press.

Branford, J. D., Brown, A., & Cocking, R. (Eds.). (2000). *How people learn: Brain, mind, experience, and school.* Washington, DC: National Research Council.

Burns, M. (1998). *Math: Facing an American phobia.* Sausalito, CA: Math Solutions Publications.

Burns, M. (2000). *About teaching mathematics: A K–8 resource.* Sausalito, CA: Math Solutions Publications.

Business Coalition for Education Reform. (1998). *The formula for success: A business leader's guide to supporting math and science achievement.* Washington, DC: U.S. Department of Education.

Carpenter, T. P., Fennema, E., Loef Franke, M., Levi, L., & Empson, S. B. (1999). *Children's mathematics: Cognitively guided instruction.* Portsmouth, NH: Heinemann.

Clements, D., & Sarama, J. (2004). *Engaging young children in mathematics: Standards for early childhood mathematics education.* Mahwah, NJ: Lawrence Erlbaum.

Donovan, S., & Bransford, J. (2005). *How students learn mathematics in the classroom.* Washington, DC: National Academy Press.

Essential Learnings Framework 1. (2003). Retrieved December 26, 2006, from http://www.education.tas.gov.au/school/educators/curriculum/elscurriculum/els1.pdf

Fosnot, C., & Dolk, M. (2001). *Young mathematicians at work: Constructing number sense, addition and subtraction.* Portsmouth, NH: Heinemann.

Fountas, I., & Pinnell, G. S. (2000). *Guiding readers and writers (Grade 3–6): Teaching comprehension, genre, and content literacy.* Portsmouth, NH: Heinemann.

Ginsberg, H. P. (1989). *Children's arithmetic: How they learn it and how you teach it* (2nd ed.). Austin, TX: PRO-ED.

Glickman, C. D. (2003). *Holding sacred ground.* San Francisco: Jossey-Bass.

Hersh, R. (1997). *What is mathematics, really?* New York: Oxford University Press.

Hiebert, J. (1997). *Making sense: Teaching and learning mathematics with understanding.* Portsmouth, NH: Heinemann.

Kamii, C. (1989). *Young children continue to reinvent arithmetic, 2nd grade.* New York: Teachers College Press.

Ma, L. (1999). *Knowing and teaching elementary mathematics.* Mahwah, NJ: Lawrence Erlbaum.

Marzano, R. J., Pickering, D. J., & Pollock, J. E. (2001). *Classroom instruction that works: Research-based studies for increasing student achievement.* Alexandria, VA: Association for Supervision and Curriculum Development.

McTighe, J., & O'Conner, K. (2005). Seven practices for effective learning. *Educational Leadership: Assessment to Promote Learning, 63*(3), 10–17.

National Council of Teachers of Mathematics. (1989). *Curriculum and evaluation standards for school mathematics.* Reston, VA: National Council of Teachers of Mathematics.

National Council of Teachers of Mathematics. (1993). *Research ideas for the classroom.* Reston, VA: National Council of Teachers of Mathematics.

National Council of Teachers of Mathematics. (2000). *Principles and standards for school mathematics.* Reston, VA: National Council of Teachers of Mathematics.

National Council of Teachers of Mathematics. (2002). *Putting research into practice in the elementary grades.* Reston, VA: National Council of Teachers of Mathematics.

National Council of Teachers of Mathematics. (2003). *Research companion to principles and standards for school mathematics.* Reston, VA: National Council of Teachers of Mathematics.

National Research Council. (1989). *Everybody counts.* Washington, DC: National Academy of Sciences.

National Research Council. (2001). *Adding it up: Helping children learn mathematics.* Washington, DC: National Academy Press.

National Research Council. (2002). *Helping children learn mathematics.* Washington, DC: National Academy Press.

National Research Council. (2005). *How students learn: Mathematics in the classroom.* Washington, DC: National Academy Press.

Paulos, J. A. (1988). *Innumeracy: Mathematical illiteracy and its consequences.* New York: Vintage Books.

Paulos, J. A. (1991). *Beyond numeracy.* New York: Vintage Books.

Rose, C., Minton, L., & Arline, C. (2006). *Uncovering student thinking in mathematics: 25 formative assessment probes.* Thousand Oaks, CA: Corwin Press.

Scharer, P. L., Pinnell, G. S., Lyons, C., & Fountas, I. (2005). Becoming an engaged reader [Electronic version]. *Educational Leadership, 65*(2), 25–29.

Simon, M. (1995). Restructuring mathematics pedagogy from a constructivist perspective. *Journal for Research in Mathematics Education, 26,* 114–145.

Steen, L. A. (1998). Numeracy: The new literacy for a data-drenched society. *Educational Leadership, 57*(2), 8–13.

Tripp, D. (1993). *Critical incidents in teaching: Developing professional judgement.* London: Routledge.

United States Department of Education. (2004, October). *A guide to education and* No Child Left Behind. Retrieved February 28, 2006, from http://www.ed.gov/nclb/overview/intro/guide/guide_pg11.html

United States Department of Education. (2006, February). *Math now: Advancing math education in elementary and middle school.* Retrieved December 18, 2006, from http://www.ed.gov/about/inits/ed/competitiveness/math-now.html

Yackel, E., Cobb, P., Wood, T., Wheatley, G., & Merkel, G. (1990). *The importance of social interaction in children's construction of mathematical knowledge.* Reston, VA: National Council of Teachers of Mathematics.

Index